SMASHING
Photoshop
CS5

PUBLISHER'S ACKNOWLEDGMENTS

Some of the people who helped bring this book to market include the following:

Editorial and Production
VP Consumer and Technology Publishing Director: Michelle Leete
Associate Director— Book Content Management: Martin Tribe
Associate Publisher: Chris Webb
Publishing Assistant: Ellie Scott
Project Editor: Juliet Booker
Development Editor: Kezia Endsley
Technical Editor: Tom Ross
Copy Editor: Abigail Saffrey

Marketing
Senior Marketing Manager: Louise Breinholt
Marketing Executive: Katherine Parrett

Composition Services
Compositor: Indianapolis Composition Services
Proof Reader: Gareth Haman
Indexer: Potomac Indexing LLC

SMASHING
Photoshop
CS5

100 PROFESSIONAL TECHNIQUES

Sue Jenkins

WILEY

A John Wiley and Sons, Ltd, Publication

This edition first published 2010
© 2010 John Wiley & Sons, Ltd.

Registered office
John Wiley & Sons Ltd, The Atrium, Southern Gate, Chichester, West Sussex, PO19 8SQ,
United Kingdom

For details of our global editorial offices, for customer services and for information about
how to apply for permission to reuse the copyright material in this book please see our
website at www.wiley.com.

The right of the author to be identified as the author of this work has been asserted in
accordance with the Copyright, Designs and Patents Act 1988.

Wiley also publishes its books in a variety of electronic formats. Some content that
appears in print may not be available in electronic books.

Adobe and Photoshop are registered trademarks of Adobe Systems, Inc.

Designations used by companies to distinguish their products are often claimed as
trademarks. All brand names and product names used in this book are trade names,
service marks, trademarks or registered trademarks of their respective owners. The
publisher is not associated with any product or vendor mentioned in this book. This
publication is designed to provide accurate and authoritative information in regard to
the subject matter covered. It is sold on the understanding that the publisher is not
engaged in rendering professional services. If professional advice or other expert
assistance is required, the services of a competent professional should be sought.

978-0-470-66153-6

A catalogue record for this book is available from the British Library.

Printed in the USA by CJ Krehbiel Company

To Phil and Kyle for their laughter, patience, and frequent squeezes. — Sue Jenkins

Acknowledgments

A generous heaping helping of thanks to my literary agent Matt Wagner and associate publisher Chris Webb; to project editor Juliet Booker, development editor Kezia Endsley, and technical editor Tom Ross; to publishing assistant Ellie Scott; and to everyone in marketing and composition services at Wiley/Smashing Magazine who helped with the production of this gorgeous full-color edition.

About the Author

Sue Jenkins is a web designer, graphic designer, illustrator, fine art photographer (www.suejenkinsphotography.com), software instructor, writer, and the owner of the Luckychair (www.luckychair.com), a professional design studio serving companies across the U.S.A. since 1997. Sue is the author of several books on Adobe software and design including *Dreamweaver All-in-One For Dummies, Web Design All-in-One For Dummies, Web Design: The L-Line, The Express Line to Learning,* and *How To Do Everything Illustrator.* She is also the award-winning software instructor in six of ClassOnDemand's (www.classondemand.com) Adobe Training DVDs: *Dreamweaver for Designers* (winner of a 2007 Bronze Telly Award), *Designer's Guide to Photoshop, Designer's Guide to Illustrator* (winner of a 2009 Annual Communicator Award of Distinction), *Fundamentals of Photoshop Elements* (winner of a 2009 DV Magazine Award of Excellence), *Complete Training for Adobe Dreamweaver CS5,* and *Complete Training for Adobe Photoshop CS5.* In addition, Sue is an Adobe Certified Expert/ Adobe Certified Instructor teaching three-day courses in Dreamweaver, Illustrator, and Photoshop at Noble Desktop (www.nobledesktop.com) in New York City, and is currently working toward her MFA in Photography. Sue lives with her husband and son in Pennsylvania, U.S.A.

Contents

CONTENTS

PART V: SPECIAL EFFECTS 267

PART VI: IMAGE DISTRESSING 327

PART VII: IMAGE RETOUCHING AND RESTORATION 367

CONTENTS

Introduction

Yippie! I am thrilled that you picked up this book because it's loaded with 100 creative and innovative ideas to help jumpstart your creativity and teach you to do more with your designs and photographs, faster and better, with Photoshop. After flipping through the pages, you'll soon discover how valuable an addition this book will be to your art and design library.

What makes this particular tutorial book special is that it's a reference guide designed to let you jump from chapter to chapter so you can read and learn about the things that interest you as the need arises. Think of each of these 100 chapters as their own little reference zones where you'll learn about how to perform specific tasks using a variety of tools, filters, styles, adjustment layers, and more, to achieve your specific goals.

Everything you find in this book is written simply and clearly, so you don't have to wade through complicated technical help files or have to commit anything to memory. In each chapter, you'll find detailed, step-by-step, easy-to-follow instructions, along with helpful tips and links to pages on SmashingMagazine.com and other websites where you can download special custom brushes, patterns, fonts, and textures. As you work through the chapters, you'll learn new ways to do familiar things like accessing commands, tools, and keyboard shortcuts, as well as gain new insight about how the program works to enhance your personal creative workflow.

Photoshop is the number one image-editing software tool available today and with good reason. On February 19th, 2010, Adobe Photoshop celebrated its 20th anniversary and throughout that entire time it has remained on the cutting edge of technology and creative innovation. I've personally been a Photoshop user since early 1990, and over the years I've witnessed firsthand how this amazing software has helped to change not only how we think about photography and design, but how we work. Today, Photoshop is used worldwide by professional web designers, graphic designers, video designers, digital artists, photographers, and artists, as well art students, amateur photographers, videographers, and budding creative types.

Whatever your particular creative interest is in using Photoshop, this book is for you. The bottom line is that I want to make you comfortable with performing tasks in Photoshop in the hopes that you'll turn to this book often as a springboard for sparking new ideas and gaining inspiration for all your projects.

To learn more about me, my photography, and my other books and DVDs, visit www. luckychair.com and www.suejenkinsphotography.com.

To learn more about Photoshop's 20th anniversary, visit www.photoshop20anniversary.com.

WEB LAYOUT AND OPTIMIZATION

TECHNIQUE 1

SETTING UP A GRID

NO DOUBT YOU'VE already heard about how important it is to design your print and web layouts using the grid system. A good grid-based layout not only keeps your content neat and organized, but also allows you to add new content and information into your layout in a logical and visually pleasing manner. Of course, the old caveat still applies that rules are meant to be broken, but you can't break the rules until you know how to follow them. Here you'll learn how to setup a 960-pixel web grid in Photoshop. Once you learn the technique, you can create grids for all your print and web projects.

INTERNET HINT: To generate your own custom CSS grid, which you can then take a screenshot of and use as a template in Photoshop, visit http://www.spry-soft.com/grids/.

STEP 1   The first thing you need to do is open a blank document in the size and format that you would like to work in. For instance, to make a web layout following a grid layout optimized for a 1024×768 monitor, you'll create a grid that is 960 pixels wide by 768 pixels tall with 12 60-pixel wide subdivisions and 11 20-pixel wide gutters (that's the spaces between the subdivisions). Select **File** > **New** to open the New document dialog box. Under Preset choose Web, which will automatically set the resolution to 72 pixels/inch and the color mode to RGB. Next, enter a width of 960 and a height of 768, and then click OK.

Next you'll make the grid visible by choosing **View** > **Show** > **Grid**. If you do not see the Show option under the View menus, select Show All Menu Items at the bottom of the View dropdown to reveal the hidden menu options. You may also toggle the grid on and off by pressing Ctrl+'/⌘+'.

STEP 2   By default, the grid appears with a gridline every inch with four subdivisions. However, you can easily adjust the grid attributes through Photoshop's Preferences. To open the Preferences dialog box, choose Ctrl+K/⌘+K and adjust the settings in the Guides, Grid & Slices category. For the purposes of this exercise, change the Gridline Every number to 40 and the unit of measure to pixels. Leave the subdivision setting at 4; this will ensure that each grid subdivision line is 10 pixels apart. This 10-pixel space will also serve as the gutter lines between major grid divisions. Click OK to save the changes and return to your document.

STEP 3   Next you'll add some vertical guides. Make sure your rulers are displaying along the top and left edges of your document window. Rulers can be toggled on and off by selecting **View** > **Rulers** or pressing Ctrl+R/⌘+R. Because you created a web document in Step 1, your rulers should be automatically set to display in pixels. If not, right+click/⌘+click on the ruler and select the desired unit from the Ruler's context menu.

To set your first vertical guide, click and drag from the left ruler toward your document window without releasing your mouse. Your cursor will change to a double-sided arrow with two vertical lines in between and you will see the outline of a vertical guide running across your screen. Position this guide along the left edge of your document and release your mouse. Guides, once released, appear as bright blue lines, which can be easily repositioned when needed using the Move tool, or locked into place using the **View** > **Guides** menu. Place another vertical guide along the right edge of your document and then add two more guides at the first 10-pixel subdivision line along both the left and right edges, as shown in Figure 1-1.

4

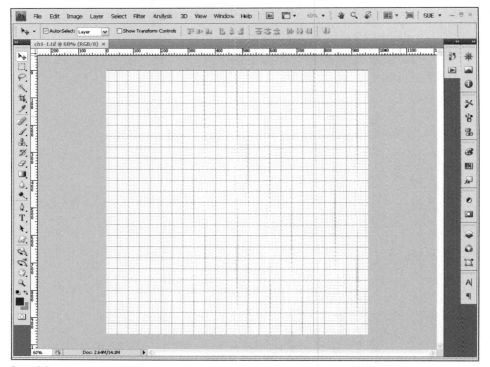

Figure 1-1

To more quickly add the guides to your file, next you'll create a rectangle shape to serve as your template. With your Info panel visible (so you can see the W and H attributes of your selection), use the Rectangular Marquis tool to drag out a shape that is 60 pixels wide by 768 pixels tall. To fill this selection with a color, release your mouse and press the Create New Fill or Adjustment Layer button (it looks like a black and white cookie) at the bottom of your Layers panel, choose Solid Color from the menu, and from the Color Picker dialog box, select a soft color that won't distract from your layout, such as a pale yellow or very light blue.

Add a vertical guide along the right edge of this shape, and then add two more at the next two 10-pixel subdivision lines to the shape's right edge. You're going to repeat this process to add rectangular shapes and vertical guides until the entire document is filled up. To make duplicate rectangles quickly, drag and drop the rectangular shape layer onto the panel's Create New Layer button or choose Duplicate Layer from the layer's context menu. Move each new layer into position along your grid and add guides in between, as seen in Figure 1-2.

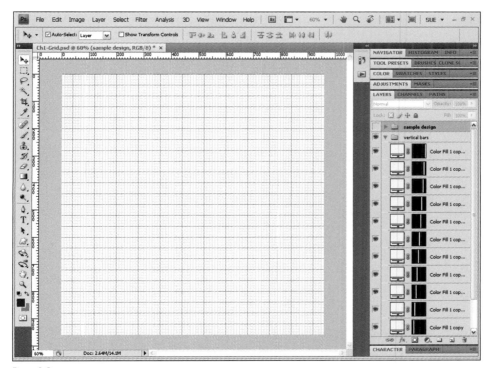

Figure 1-2

STEP 4 Now that you have your grid system in place, you're ready to create your layout. Use the guides and gutters to lay out your content. As long as you follow the margins created by the guidelines, you should be able to create a visually pleasing and interesting layout. For example, in the layout shown in Figure 1-3, I've added content placeholders for the logo/navigation, a rotating banner area, a row of special items, a place for the latest news, and a section for quick links.

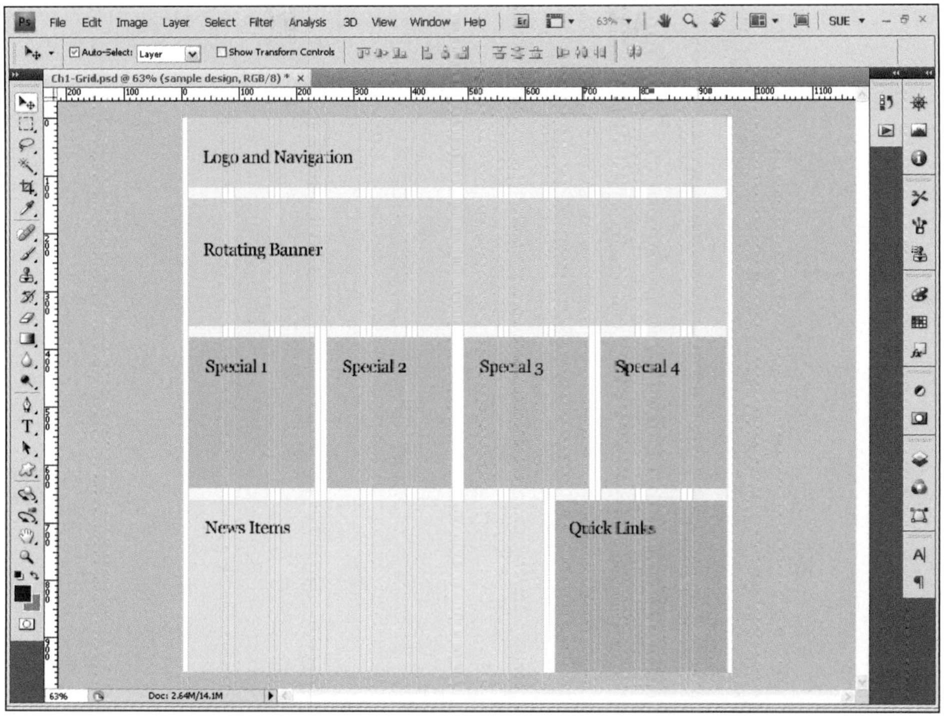
Ch1-Grid.psd @ 63% (sample design, RGB/8) *
Logo and Navigation
Rotating Banner
Special 1
Special 2
Special 3
Special 4
News Items
Quick Links

Figure 1-3

TECHNIQUE

2

MAKING CUSTOM PATTERNS

YES, PHOTOSHOP'S PATTERN libraries include dozens of interesting patterns that you can use to fill selected areas of your designs. But what should you do when you need a different pattern that will precisely fit into your specific design? Make one yourself, of course! Designing your own patterns in Photoshop is super easy once you know the basics of pattern design and how to create seamless repeats using the Offset Filter.

Custom patterns can be created with either a square or rectangular layout. In this exercise you'll learn how to create a simple square format web pattern from a preset Photoshop shape. Later, on your own, you can use these same steps to create custom patterns from your own designs.

HINT: Keep in mind that once you add a pattern in Photoshop, its attributes cannot be changed. Therefore, always save the file you used to create the pattern in case you want to create new, similar patterns with different colors, sizes, effects, and so on.

STEP 1 Press Ctrl+N/⌘−N to launch the New dialog box and create a new Web document with the dimensions of 300×300 pixels. Once the document opens, use the Color panel to set your foreground and background colors to any two colors you find appealing. For example, you might set your foreground to white and your background to a purple with the hex value of #632c82.

STEP 2 Press U to select the Custom Shape tool from your toolbar (or press Shift+U until you have it), make sure that the Shape Layers option is selected on the Options bar, and then click on the Custom Shape Picker drop-down menu at the top of your screen. You need to access a shape from another shape library, so click the Pattern pop-up panel menu to view the list of available shape libraries. Select Ornaments and, when the dialog box opens asking whether you want to replace the current shapes with the shapes from ornaments, press

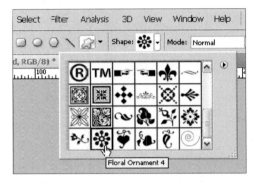

Figure 2-1

the Append button. Scroll down in the Custom Shape Picker to the bottom of the ornaments and select the design called Floral Ornament 4, as shown in Figure 2-1.

STEP 3 Drag out a medium-sized floral ornament shape onto the center of your document while pressing the Shift key to constrain proportions, and then release your mouse. Press V to switch your cursor to the Move tool and reposition the shape so that it is centered inside your document window. If necessary, use the arrow keys, guides, rulers, and alignment tools to fine-tune the shape's placement. Figure 2-2 shows an example of how this might look.

Figure 2-2

9

STEP 4   If you were to make a pattern of this design as it exists now, it would look nice but be a little boring, as the shapes would automatically line up in a neat symmetrical, grid-like fashion, like the example in Figure 2-3. To add a little more dynamism to the pattern, duplicate the shape layer by dragging the shape layer onto the Create a New Layer button found on the Layers panel.

Figure 2-3

STEP 5   Now comes the interesting part. Select **Filter > Other > Offset** to open the Offset dialog box. If you can't see the Other menu option, click Show All Menu Items. The selected shape layer must be rasterized before you can use the offset filter, so when the alert dialog box appears, click the OK button. Make sure the Undefined Areas is set to Wrap Around and then set the horizontal and vertical fields to half the document's dimensions. For example, this file is 300×300 pixels, which means you'll want to set each of the fields to 150 pixels. If the Preview button is checked, you should now see how your rasterized layer has been quartered with each piece placed into one of the document's four corners, while your original shape layer is still displaying in the center of your document window, as shown in Figure 2-4. Click OK to close the Offset dialog box.

Figure 2-4

STEP 6   Now you'll add your pattern to Photoshop. Press Ctrl+A/⌘+A to select the entire document and select **Edit > Define Pattern**. When the Pattern Name dialog box appears, give your new pattern a name (such as *Bloboids*) and click OK. Your new pattern is now saved and can be used at any time! To see how your new pattern looks, open a new 600×600-pixel Web document, click the Create New Fill or Adjustment Layer button on the Layers panel, select Pattern from the top of the pop-up menu, and when the Pattern Fill dialog box appears, click the arrow on the Pattern Picker button to select your new pattern. Click OK and you're done. Patterns can be used to fill an entire document window or any selected shape, like the heart in Figure 2-5.

Figure 2-5

11

CREATING BACKGROUND TILES

INSTEAD OF HAVING a boring solid color background on your next Web project, consider using a photographic background tile. When used with care, background tiles can be an unusual and memorable feature of a well-designed site.

To create your background tile, you'll combine some of the skills you learned in Technique #2,

"Making Custom Patterns," with new skills using the Crop and Clone Stamp tools. Tiles can be rectangular or square, depending on your needs and the size of the original file. Bear in mind, however, that larger rectangular tiles tend to hide the internal offset seams best. For this technique, you'll be creating a large rectangular tile from a photo of the ocean.

INTERNET HINT: Take a look at Carsonified.com and BrightCreative.com for good examples of tiling backgrounds. Or if you're feeling lazy and looking for more of a vector graphic vibe for your site, check out some of the free tiles at http://www. squidfingers.com/patterns/.

STEP 1   Select **File > Open** to open a digital photograph in your Photoshop workspace. If your original photograph is a high-resolution JPG file, you'll need to scale it down for the Web. Select **Image > Image Size** to open the Image Size dialog box. Adjust the Resolution to 72 pixels/inch and set the width to 700 px. This will automatically resize the image's pixel dimensions. For example, if your original photo has a resolution of 300 and pixel dimensions of 3008×2000, after adjusting the resolution and width, the new pixel dimensions will be 700×460. Figure 3-1 shows the image for this exercise after it has been resized.

Figure 3-1

STEP 2   Because this technique requires you to use the offset filter to convert your image into a tile, both the image dimensions need to be divisible by 2. Select the Crop tool from the toolbar, click the Front Image button on the Control bar to view the document's current dimensions, and adjust the Height to 460 pixels. Next, drag the Crop tool across the area you want to crop and click Enter or Return. Your image will now be 700 pixels wide and 460 pixels high.

STEP 3   Select **Filter > Other > Offset** to open the Offset dialog box. (If you can't see the Other menu option, click Show All Menu Items.) Set the Horizontal field to 350 and Vertical field to 230 pixels, which is half this document's dimensions, set the Undefined Areas to Wrap Around, and click OK. Figure 3-2 illustrates how your image should appear after applying the offset filter.

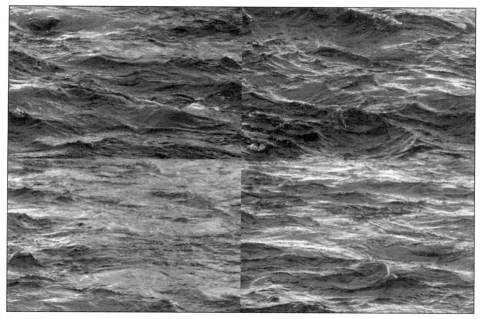

Figure 3-2

STEP 4   From the toolbar, select the Clone Stamp tool (S), set the tool's brush to 0% hardness on the Options bar, and open the Clone Source panel by selecting **Window > Clone Source**. Deselect the Show Overlay option in the panel, place your Clone Source tool above a section of the document without a visible seam, and press the Alt/Option button as you click once on your document to sample the image. Release the Alt/Option button and then paint away the seams by clicking and dragging the tool across an area of your image with a visible seam. The idea here is to use the Clone Stamp tool to cover up the interior seams in as realistic a manner as possible. Sample and paint using this tool as many times as needed to achieve the desired effect. Figure 3-3 shows an example of the image after using the Clone Stamp tool.

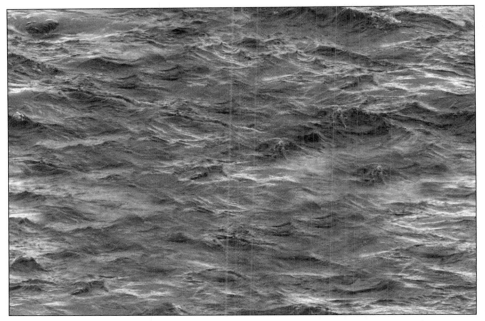

Figure 3-3

STEP 5 Save your new Web tile as a JPG file by selecting **File > Save For Web & Devices**. When the dialog box opens, adjust the settings on the right side of the panel to get the file size as close to below 50 KB as possible without losing too much of the image quality, and then click OK to save the JPG on your computer in the location of your choice.

STEP 6 To see how your new tile looks in a browser window, all you really need to do is create a simple Web page with a background image style in the CSS, as in the following code example:

```
<html>
<head>
<title>Untitled</title>
<style type="text/css">
body {
    background-image: url(images/tile_oceanwaves.jpg);
}
</style>
</head>

<body>
</body>
</html>
```

Take a look at Figure 3-4 for an example of how a Web page using this particular tile appears in a browser window.

Figure 3-4

TECHNIQUE

4

CREATING SEMI-TRANSPARENT RIBBONS

ONE OF THE best ways to add dimensionality to your web layouts is to include 3D effects like drop shadows, beveled edges, and layered transparency. In this exercise, you learn how to draw overlapping bubbles and ribbons of color with the Ellipse and Pen tools and then modify the blending mode and transparency of each to create dynamic 3D effects for your layouts.

STEP 1 Select **File > New** to open the New document dialog box. Under Preset choose Web, set the width to 960, the height to 768, and click OK.

STEP 2 Select the Pen tool and use the Shape Layers setting on the Control bar to ensure that you'll be drawing closed shapes with editable color fills. Using the Pen tool, draw a ribbon-like closed shape, like the one shown in Figure 4-1. Don't worry too much about being perfect as you draw; you can always adjust the curves and anchor points using the Direct Selection tool (A) after closing the shape. With a shape layer, you can easily adjust the color of your new shape through the Layers panel.

> INTERNET HINT: *Need to brush up on your Pen tool skills? Try this resource:* *http://psdfan.com/tutorials/drawing/become-a-master-of-the-pen-tool-in-under-30-minutes/.*

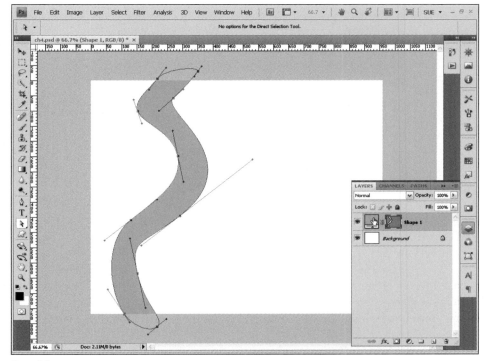

Figure 4-1

STEP 3 Next, draw a second, similar shape slightly overlapping the first one. To see how this second shape interacts with the first one, adjust the second shape's opacity down to about 80%, as illustrated in Figure 4-2.

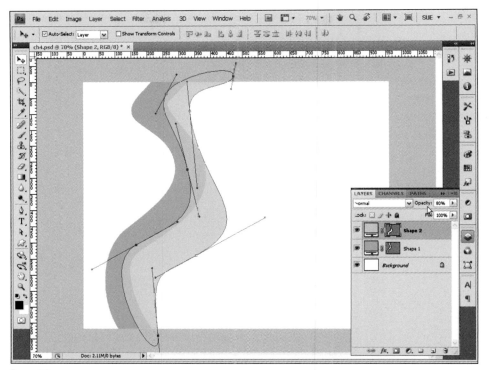

Figure 4-2

STEP 4 To create the 3D overlapping soft shadow effect, apply the Inner Glow Layer Style to the second shape using the Layer Style button at the bottom of the Layers panel. When the Layer Style dialog box opens, change the blending mode color to a dark gray, adjust the opacity down to about 50%, and set the blending mode to Multiply. To deepen the shadow effect, adjust the choke and size to your liking. For instance, you might set the choke to 23% and the size to 10 px.

STEP 5 To add further definition, give your shape a 1–2 px light gray stroke and add a gradient overlay using the Screen blending mode with an opacity set to about 40%. If desired, adjust the angle to set the direction of the gradient to your liking. Click OK to save these settings. Your image should now look something like the example shown in Figure 4-3.

STEP 6 Next, copy this layer's style by right+clicking/⌘+clicking on the layer's Layer Style *fx.* icon and selecting Copy Layer Style from the layer's context menu. To paste this layer style onto your first shape, select the first shape's layer and choose the Paste Layer Style option from the layer's context menu.

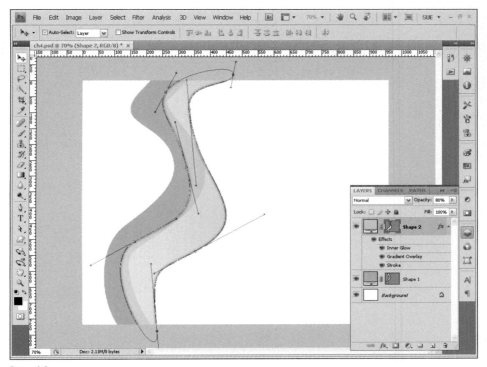

Figure 4-3

STEP 7   Continue creating additional ribbon shapes as needed following this same method as well as circular shapes using the Ellipse tool, changing the color, blending mode, opacity, and other settings as desired, as illustrated in Figure 4-4. Feel free to improvise and don't be afraid to speed things along by duplicating any existing shape layer and then adjusting the new layer's attributes through the Layers panel.

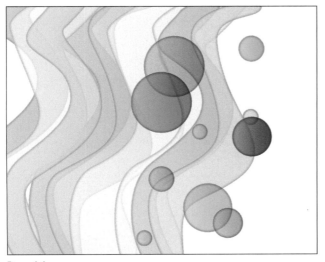

Figure 4-4

TECHNIQUE

5

CREATING INSET LINES

SEPARATING SECTIONS OF a Web or print layout often involves adding horizontal and vertical divider lines. While a simple 1 or 2 px line can look crisp and clean in some designs, in others it just looks unpolished and graphically uninteresting. For those times, try working with inset lines instead. Inset lines give the subtle illusion of a slight indentation or embossing between two sections, making it appear that the sections in your layout are physically detachable. For instance, you might try using inset lines to separate your Website's navigation links, as detailed in this technique.

STEP 1   Select **File** > **New** to open the New document dialog box. Under Preset choose Web, set the width to 960, the height to 30, and click OK. Next, click the Add New Fill or Adjustment Layer button at the bottom of the Layers panel, choose Solid Color, and fill the entire document with a forest green color, such as #2b543f.

STEP 2   Select the Type tool, set the font to Georgia, 14 pt, white, and type the following words in a single line with 10 spaces (and no commas) between each word: Home, History, Services, Projects, Contact. Position the line of text about 20 px in from the left edge of the document window, as shown in Figure 5-1.

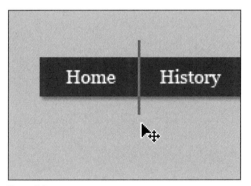

Figure 5-1

STEP 3   Create a vertical divider by selecting the Rectangle tool (U) and drawing a black, 1 px wide, vertical rectangle between the words Home and History that slightly extends vertically past the bounds of the document, as illustrated in Figure 5-2. Extending past the document's edges like this helps ensure that the inset line effect looks crisp from top to bottom, rather than appearing as if one of its edges is cut off.

Figure 5-2

STEP 4   With your new shape layer selected, choose **Layer** > **Layer Style** > **Drop Shadow**. In the Layer Style dialog box that opens, change the drop shadow color to white, the blending mode to Soft Light, the distance to 1 px, and the size to 1 px. Then click OK.

> HINT: *For a more dramatic inset line, try using a different blending mode for the drop shadow, such as Normal or Color Dodge, or adjust the drop shadow color to a hue that's complementary to the document background.*

STEP 5   To finish the layout, duplicate the shape layer four times and position each layer to the right of the remaining words in the document, as shown in Figure 5-3. Inset lines look great on navigation bars, Web ads, Web layouts, and print layouts.

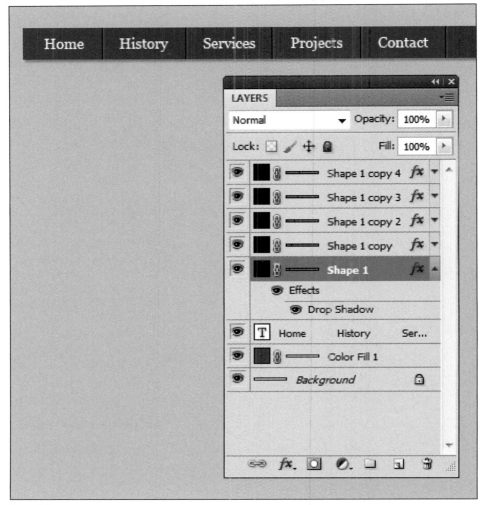

Figure 5-3

23

CUTTING A ZIGZAG EDGE

THESE DAYS IT seems like every Web 2.0 layout uses the same kind of slick color bands to section off the various parts of a Website, so you can visually identify the header and footer from the body of the layout. While these types of graphic divisions are useful from a user interface standpoint, they don't need to look so boring.

Make your layouts stand out from the crowd by adding a customized design element, such as a zigzag, a scallop, or other custom shape, to your section edges. In this technique, you'll learn how easy it is to add an interesting zigzag design element to the footer of your Web layout.

STEP 1   Select **File** > **New** to open the New document dialog box. Under Preset choose Web, set the width to 960, the height to 300, and click OK. The background color of your layout can be any color you like, either with or without a texture. For instance, you might set the background to a tan color with a hexadecimal value of #e3ddcb or add a stone texture background.

STEP 2   To create the color divider for the footer area, set the foreground color in your toolbar to a maroon color with the hexadecimal value of #500809, select the Rectangle tool from the toolbar, and draw a rectangular shape that is 960 px wide by 70 px tall across the bottom of your layout, as shown in the example in Figure 6-1.

Figure 6-1

STEP 3   The zigzag pattern must now be created in a separate file. Select **File** > **New** to open the New document dialog box. Under Preset choose Web, set the width to 12, the height to 7, and click OK. When the new file opens, zoom in to 3200% so you can see the file up close. Click the Create New Fill or Adjustment Layer button on the Layers panel and add a solid color adjustment layer to your file. When the color picker appears, set the color to the same maroon color with a hex value #500809 and click OK.

STEP 4 Next you'll edit out some of the Color Fill layer's mask to create the zigzag shape. Press D on your keyboard to reset the foreground and background colors to black and white, select the layer mask thumbnail of your Color Fill layer in the Layers panel, and—using the Pencil tool with a radius set to 1—erase some of the pixels so that your mask looks like the triangle shape in Figure 6-2. When you're finished, click away from the layer mask in the Layers panel to deselect the mask.

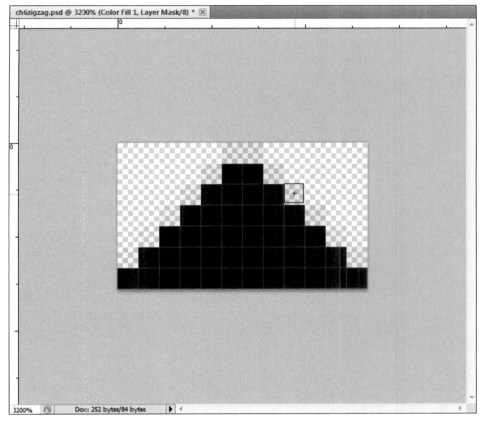

Figure 6-2

STEP 5 Press Ctrl+A/⌘+A to select the entire document's contents and then select **Edit > Define Pattern**. When the Pattern Name dialog box appears, name your pattern Zigzag and click OK.

To save this zigzag graphic file for later use (for instance, you might want to use it again in another color), press Ctrl+S/⌘+S so you can name the file and save it in your desired location.

STEP 6 To add the new pattern to your original file, use the Rectangular Marquee tool to drag out a 960×7 px sized rectangular shape across the top edge of the maroon colored section in your file. (This size is important so make sure you rectangle is exactly 960×7 px.) For help making precise selections, look to the Width and Height fields on the Info panel (F8). After releasing your mouse, click the Create New Fill or Adjustment Layer button at the bottom of the Layers panel and select Pattern from the context menu.

Your new zigzag pattern should automatically fill your selection, however it might not fill the space as cleanly as you'd like it to, as illustrated in Figure 6-3.

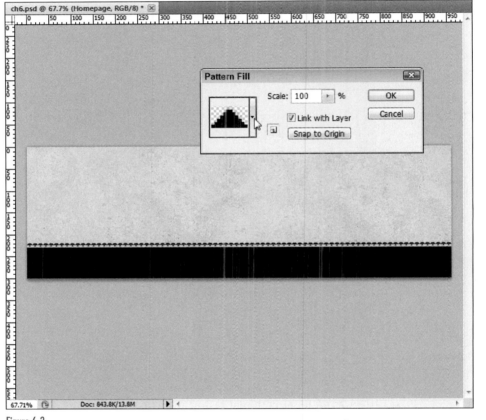

Figure 6-3

With the Pattern Fill dialog box still open, adjust how the pattern sits within the layer mask by clicking and dragging on the pattern within your document window until the bottom of the pattern is aligned within the mask space, as shown in Figure 6-4. When you have the pattern aligned properly, click OK to close the dialog box.

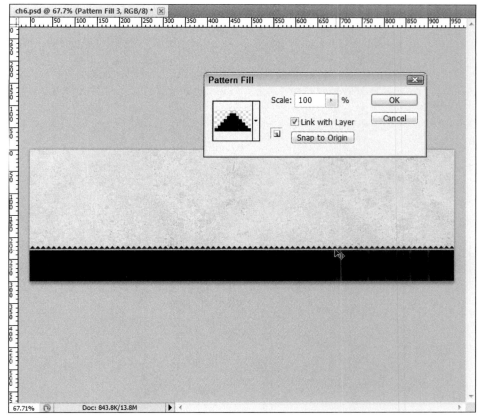

Figure 6-4

STEP 7 Use the Move tool (V) to position the pattern layer at the top edge of the maroon section. Et voila! You have a fancy zigzag edge.

To further enhance this design element, merge the maroon rectangle and pattern layer by selecting both layers in the Layers panel and pressing Ctrl+E/⌘+E, and then apply layer styles through the Layers panel, such as a Drop Shadow, Stroke, and Gradient Overlay, for added definition and flair. Figure 6-5 shows an example of the zigzag design.

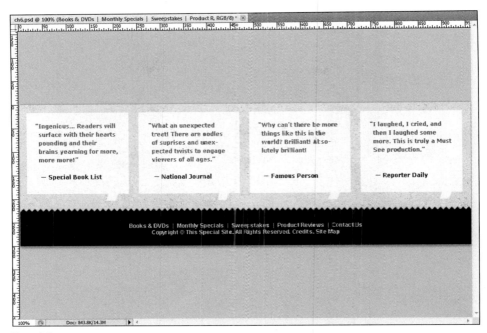

Figure 6-5

CREATING A FAVICON

A *FAVICON* IS a customizable, 16×16 px, 256-color icon that uses the Windows Icon (.ico) file extension. When uploaded to the root directory of a Website, this tiny graphic appears in your browser window to the left of the URL in the Location or Address Bar, next to the name of any page tabs and saved Websites in your list of "favorites" in certain browsers, as the icon on your iPhone, and as the icon for any Internet shortcuts you may have placed on your computer desktop. For instance, the *Smashing Magazine* Website favicon is a tiny white S on an orange-red background, as shown in Figure 7-1.

Figure 7-1

Fortunately, creating the graphic and adding it to a Web page is super easy—especially when you have the free ICO Windows Icon file format plug-in for Photoshop from Telegraphics.com.au and you know enough HTML to add a line of code to the <head> area of your pages. To design, create, and install a favicon on your own (or your client's) Website, follow the steps outlined here.

STEP 1   Start by downloading the free (although donations are accepted) Windows Icon Photoshop plug-in from the Telegraphics Website at http://www.telegraphics.com.au/ sw/#icoformat. After downloading the file, install the plug-in and restart Photoshop.

STEP 2   Within Photoshop, select **File > New** to open the New document dialog box. Under Preset choose Web, and since a 16×16 px file might be way too tiny to work with, set the width and height to 64, and then click OK.

STEP 3   If you already have a logo or other graphic element that you'd like to use for the favicon, paste that graphic into the document and resize it to fit within the canvas. Then select **Image > Image Size** to open the Image Size dialog box, set the width and height to 16 px, and click OK.

If the image looks good at the reduced size, proceed to Step 4. For example, Figure 7-2 shows a side-by-side comparison of a graphic at 64×64 px (left) next to the same file reduced to 16×16 px (right).

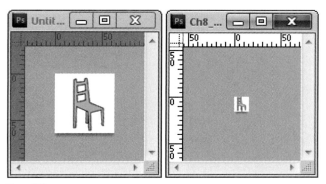

Figure 7-2

Otherwise, if the image looks too fuzzy or just not quite right, undo the resize (Ctrl+Z/⌘+Z), edit the image as needed, and try resizing again. You may need to simplify the graphic, apply a sharpening filter, increase the contrast, and/or add more saturation to get the file to look good at the smaller size. Be patient; you'll get it.

STEP 4   To save the 16×16 px graphic as a favicon, select **File > Save As** to open the Save As dialog box. Navigate to the location on your computer that you want to save the file into, name your graphic favicon, select ICO (Windows Icon) (*.ico) from the Format menu, and choose Save.

> INTERNET HINT: *To convert any GIF, JPG, or PNG graphic into a favicon.ico file* without *the Photoshop ICO plug-in, use the free online Favicon Generator tool at http://www.graphicsguru.com/favicon.php.*

STEP 5   Next, you will add a reference to the favicon in each page on your site on which you'd like the icon to appear. Open your Web pages, one at a time, in your preferred Web editor and add the following line of code (which can be typed on the same line) to the <head>…</head> section of the page:

```
<link rel="shortcut icon" type="image/x-icon"
          href="/favicon.ico" />
```

This line of code ensures that the browser being used to view the site can locate and display the specified favicon file. If desired, you may upload the favicon graphic to another location on your server. However, if you do that, be sure to also update the link accordingly. For example, you could place the favicon graphic inside a folder called *images*, as in:

```
<link rel="shortcut icon" type="image/x-icon"
          href="/images/favicon.ico" />
```

Unfortunately, not all browsers understand this particular link syntax. To make sure all the major browsers can use your favicon graphic, add another line of code to your HTML files, which uses alternate rel (relationship) and type attribute values:

```
<link rel="shortcut icon" type="image/x-icon"
        href="/favicon.ico" />
<link rel="icon" type="image/ico"
        href="/favicon.ico" />
```

> HINT: Many browsers, such as Firefox and Opera, no longer require the use of the .ico file format. Instead you can use a PNG file (which supports transparency) or GIF file (including animated GIFs), so long as you update the HTML code to reflect the type and location of the favicon graphic, as in these examples:

```
<link rel="icon" type="image/gif" href="/favicon.gif" />
```

> Or

```
<link rel="icon" type="image/png" href="/favicon.png" />
```

> Visit http://www.luckychair.com to view an example of an animated favicon, and then turn to Technique #8 to learn how to create it.

STEP 6 Using your preferred FTP program (such as WS-FTP, FileZilla, Fetch, or CuteFTP) or the built-in FTP feature of your HTML or Web editor, upload the new favicon graphic and the updated page(s) to the root level (or other preferred location) of your hosted Website. That's it!

To see your new favicon graphic in action, visit the domain you just modified in your favorite browser.

- If the icon appears, you've done a good job. Congratulations!
- If you don't see the icon, try refreshing the browser and/or clearing your browser's cache. If you still don't see it, verify that the favicon graphic with the .ico file extension is in the correct location on the remote server and double-check the accuracy of the link code you just added to your home page. As long as the location and link code match, the graphic should automatically appear.

> INTERNET HINT: For additional favicon ideas and inspiration, visit http://www. smashingmagazine.com/2010/03/14/50-fantastic-favicons-episode-9/

TECHNIQUE

8

CREATING AN ANIMATED FAVICON

NOW THAT YOU have learned to make a basic favicon in Technique #7, "Creating a Favicon," you're ready to create your own animated favicon. The motion in an animated favicon is created in a simple "frames-based" GIF animation, which requires no Flash and only takes a few more minutes to construct than a regular GIF favicon. Even better, all you need to make your animated favicon is Photoshop and the artwork you'll be using for the two or more "frames" of the animation.

STEP 1 Start by creating the file that holds the animation graphics. Select **File > New** to open the New document dialog box. Under Preset choose Web, set both the width and height to 16 px, and click OK.

> HINT: *If you'd prefer to work in a slightly larger file size, set the width and height to 64 px. Then, before you save the file as an animated GIF, just remember to scale the file down to 16×16.*

STEP 2 For this technique, you will need four layers: three separate graphics (one on each layer) and a 1 px border layer. Paste all the artwork you'd like to use in your animation into the open document, placing each image to be used in the animation on to its own layer, one above the other, in the order in which they should appear, starting from the bottom.

Be sure to name each layer appropriately (frame 1, frame 2, and so on) so that the animation is easy to configure. For example, in the animated GIF favicon used on the Luckychair.com Website, the file consists of four layers—one for each of the three frames of the animation, and a fourth layer called *border* that will also be visible in each frame of the animation, as illustrated in Figure 8-1.

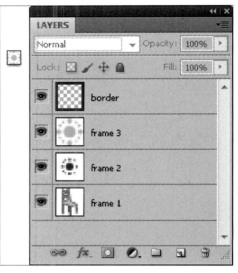

Figure 8-1

To create the border layer, select the layer called frame 3 and click the Create New Layer button at the bottom of the Layers panel. Then press Ctrl+A/⌘+A to select the entire layer, select **Edit > Stroke** to apply a 1 px inside border in the color of your choice, click OK, and name your layer *border*.

STEP 3 Select **Window > Animation** to open the Animation panel. Here is where you will set up the frames-based animation. By default, the Animation panel opens to the Animation (Timeline) view. To switch the display to the Animation (Frames) view, click the Convert to Frame Animation button in the bottom-right corner of the panel.

STEP 4 In the Animation (Frames) panel, you'll notice that the first frame of the animation is labeled with a "1" and has a time delay set to 10 seconds, which is a little too long for an animated favicon. Click on the Delay menu where it says "10 sec" and adjust the delay to 5.0 seconds.

Next, over in the Layers panel, adjust the visibility of your layers so that only the layers (frames) you want to appear in frame 1 are showing. For example, for frame 1 in the Luckychair animated favicon, the layers for frame 1 and border are visible, while the layers for frame 2 and frame 3 are hidden, as shown in Figure 8-2. This sets the scene for frame 1.

STEP 5 To add two more frames to your animation, click the Duplicates Selected Frames button at the bottom of the Animation panel twice. Then make the following adjustments to the each of the new frames:

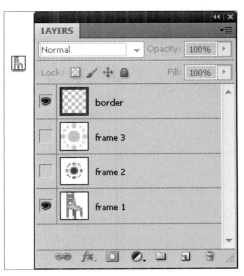

Figure 8-2

- Select frame 2, adjust the time delay to 0.2 seconds, and toggle the visibility of the layers in the Layers panel so that only the correct layers for frame 2 are visible. In other words, make frame 2 and border visible while hiding frame 1 and frame 3.

- Select frame 3, adjust the time delay to 0.2 seconds, and toggle the visibility of the layers so that frame 3 and border are visible and frames 1 and 2 are hidden.

Figure 8-3 shows how each frame in this example should be configured in the Layers panel.

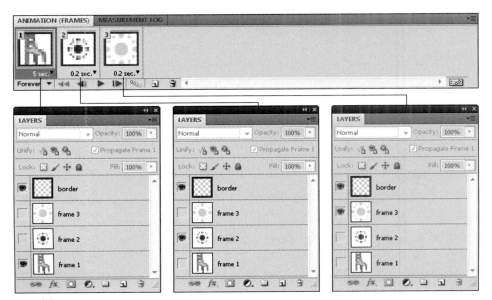

Figure 8-3

STEP 6   To preview the animation in the Animation panel before saving it, select frame 1 and press the panel's Play button. Notice that the animation plays once and then stops. Hmmm . . . that's not good. To make the animation play endlessly, adjust the playback frequency by choosing Forever from the Looping Option menu in the lower-left corner of the panel. Now try playing the animation again and you'll see the animation continuously loop. Ahhh—much better.

STEP 7   Select **File > Save For Web & Devices** to save the file as an animated GIF. When the dialog box opens, select GIF 128 No Dither from the Preset menu and click Save. Then, in the Save Optimized As dialog box, select the location where you'd like to save your file, set the filename to *favicon*, set Save as Type to Images Only, and choose Save.

> HINT: *To preview your saved animated GIF file before adding it to your Website, drag and drop the file into any open browser window.*

STEP 8   Now you are ready to use your animated GIF as a favicon. Upload the favicon.gif file to the root level of your domain and add the two lines of HTML code below to the <head>…</head> of every page on your site on which you'd like the icon to appear. After you've added the code, be sure to upload the updated pages to the server too.

```
<link rel="shortcut icon" type="image/ico" href="/favicon.ico" />
<link rel="icon" type="image/gif" href="/favicon.gif" />
```

WORKING WITH SMART OBJECTS

SMART OBJECTS ARE special Photoshop layers that contain references to original vector or raster image data, such as native Illustrator files, camera raw data, or other Photoshop images. In this technique, you'll learn how to create a simple Web ad using Smart Objects.

You can create Smart Objects in Photoshop by:

- pasting a copied Illustrator object into Photoshop (**Edit > Paste**);
- placing a file into Photoshop (**File > Place**);
- opening a file into Photoshop as a Smart Object (**File > Open As Smart Object**);
- converting one or more selected Photoshop layers into Smart Objects through the Layers panel Options menu or by using a selected layer's context menu (Convert to Smart Object).

Unlike a normal layer in Photoshop, a Smart Object layer can be edited non-destructively. Smart Objects can be repeatedly scaled, rotated, skewed, distorted, perspective transformed, and warped—all without any loss of quality as the transformations are performed on unrasterized copies of the original artwork rather than on the original file data. Although you can't adjust the pixel information (painting, erasing, and so on) of a Smart Object layer without rasterizing the layer first, there are workarounds including rasterizing and editing a duplicate layer, and editing the contents of a Smart Object layer.

STEP 1   Select **File > New** to open the New document dialog box. From Preset choose Web, set the width to 300 px, the height to 250 px, and click OK. This is a standard IAB (Interactive Advertising Bureau) size for a medium rectangular Web ad in the U.S.

STEP 2   Select **File > Place** to open the Place dialog box, and then navigate to and select a photo of your choice. Click OK. Adjust the size and position of the image as needed, and press Enter/Return to place the image into the file. Placing a file like this automatically converts the image into a Smart Object.

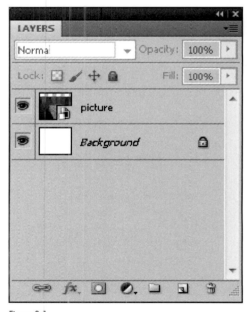

Smart Objects are easy to identify in the Layers panel by the tiny icon in the bottom-right corner of the layer's thumbnail. Typically, a Smart Object layer is labeled as "Vector Smart Object," however when placing PSD files into Photoshop, the layer's label takes on the name of the placed file, as illustrated in Figure 9-1.

Figure 9-1

STEP 3   To create an area over the photo for branding and text, use the Rectangle tool to add a 300×36 px white rectangle across the top of the file. With the Color Fill layer selected, press the Add a Layer Style button at the bottom of the panel and choose Drop Shadow. Set the distance and size to 8 px, set the angle to 90°, and click OK.

That looks good, but you can add even more of a dynamic dimensionality to the effect by separating the layer style from the layer. Choose **Layer > Layer Style > Create Layer**, and if an alert box pops up, click OK.

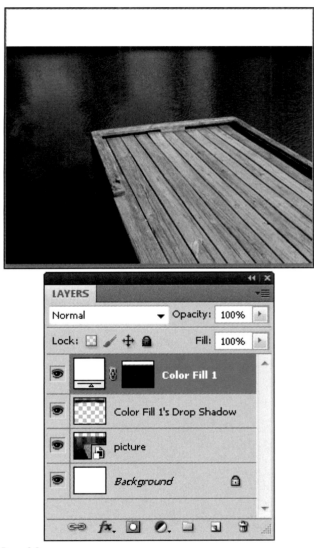

Figure 9-2

STEP 4   Next you'll place a logo and a button graphic into the file. Repeat the **File > Place** process outlined in Step 2, moving the logo graphic to the top-left corner of the document along the white bar and the button graphic to the bottom right, roughly as shown in Figure 9-3.

40

Figure 9-3

STEP 5   Now write some ad copy. Across the right side of the white bar, type **RELAXING GETAWAYS** and set the font to Arial, 16 pt, #cc9933. Then, just below the white bar, in Arial, 14 pt, #ffffff, type the words, [**PICTURE SELF HERE**]. If the white text isn't popping enough, add a drop shadow effect.

STEP 6   Even though you cannot adjust the pixels of a Smart Object without first rasterizing the image, you may still modify the image by editing the contents of that Smart Object. For instance, if your background photo needs contrast correction, you right+click/Ctrl+click on the layer and select Edit Contents from that layer's context menu. This opens the Smart Object layer (as a new file with the .psb extension) in a second Photoshop window where you can make and save your changes. Once saved, the second window closes and the adjusted Smart Object becomes part of your project.

STEP 7   To unify the design, you'll add a 1 px inside black stroke around everything. You do this by selecting the top-most layer in the Layers panel, adding a new layer above it, pressing Ctrl+A/⌘+A to select all the pixels on the new layer, and selecting **Edit > Stroke**. Be sure to save this file, as you'll use it again in Technique #10. Your ad design should now look somewhat like the example shown in Figure 9-4.

Figure 9-4

TECHNIQUE

10

USING SMART FILTERS AND EFFECTS

IN TECHNIQUE #9 you learned how to create a Web ad using Smart Objects. Here you'll take your design one step further and learn how to apply non-destructive Smart Filters, Smart Effects, and Smart Masks, all of which can be repeatedly edited at any time through the Layers panel.

STEP 1   Using the finished file you created in Technique #9, select the Smart Object picture layer inside the Layers panel. If for some reason the photo image in your file is not yet a Smart Object, select that layer and turn it into a Smart Object by choosing Convert to Smart Object from the layer's context menu or by pressing Ctrl+Alt+Shift+D/⌘+Option+Shift+D.

STEP 2   With Smart Objects, you can apply filters, effects, and masks non-destructively and then, similar to an adjustment layer, edit them at any time through the Layers panel. To see how Smart Filters work, select **Filter > Artistic > Plastic Wrap**. When the Filter Gallery dialog box opens, adjust the highlight strength to 15, the detail to 9, and the smoothness to 7, and then click OK. Figure 10-1 shows how the Plastic Wrap Smart Filter looks.

Figure 10-1

Notice in the Layers panel that the Smart Object layer now has a Plastic Wrap Smart Filter applied to it along with a blank Filter Mask. To edit the filter, double-click the filter effect name (Plastic Wrap). This reopens the Filter Gallery so you can adjust the filter sliders as needed or even apply a different filter altogether. When you're finished, click OK.

STEP 3   The Plastic Wrap filter looks dreamy as applied to the pier, but not so much for the water. To fix this, select the Smart Filters mask thumbnail right below the Smart Object layer in the Layers panel. Then press X on your keyboard to set the foreground and background colors to black and white, press B to select the Brush tool, and paint away the plastic wrap effect on the water. Painting like this effectively modifies the layer mask, allowing the Smart Filter to only show through certain areas of the mask.

STEP 4   Next you'll add a Smart Effect to create a slight vignette effect. With the photo Smart Object layer still selected, press the Add Layer Style button at the bottom of the Layers panel and choose Gradient Overlay. Adjust the opacity to 70%, the angle to 90°, and the blending mode to Overlay. Then click OK.

STEP 5   Now to make the button pop: select the button Smart Object in the Layers panel, press the Add Layer Style button at the bottom of the Layers panel, and choose Drop Shadow. Adjust the opacity to 75%, the angle to 80°, and the blending mode to Multiply. Before closing this dialog box, add a 2 px inside stroke with the hex value of #434925, and apply a smooth inner bevel with a size set to 1 and a soften set to 5. Now click OK. Figure 10-2 shows the completed Web ad.

Figure 10-2

TECHNIQUE

11

GRABBING A STILL FROM A VIDEO CLIP

EVERYONE ONLINE SEEMS to be using video these days, from YouTube and Facebook to Hulu and MySpace. Needless to say, you can find a lot of good and interesting information in a video clip. In fact, as a designer, you may occasionally need to pull a single image from a video clip to use for Websites, newsletters, or other marketing needs. Fortunately, with Photoshop Extended, pulling a still image from a video clip is easy.

STEP 1   Within Photoshop, select **File > Open** to browse for and select the video clip that contains the image you want to extract. Once selected, click the Open button to open the video file into Photoshop.

> *INTERNET HINT: You can also open a video file in Photoshop from within the Adobe Bridge application by selecting File > Open With > Adobe Photoshop CS5. To learn more about Adobe Bridge, visit: http://tv.adobe.com/show/learn-bridge-cs4/ and http://tv.adobe.com/watch/learn-adobe-bridge-cs5/what-is-adobe-bridge-cs5-.*

Acceptable QuickTime video formats for this process include MPEG-1 (.mpg or .mpeg), MPEG-4 (.mp4 or .m4v), MOV, AVI, FLV (when Adobe Flash Professional is installed), and MPEG-2 (when an MPEG-2 encoder is installed).

STEP 2   Open the Animation window by selecting **Window > Animation**. By default, the video opens in the Animation window's Timeline view (as opposed to the Frames view). Also, the entire video appears as a single video layer in the Layers panel, and the first frame in the video sequence appears in the document window.

STEP 3   Inside the Animation window, move the blue Current Time Indicator arrow to the right along the timeline until you see the frame that you'd like to capture. For example, in Figure 11-1 the Current Time Indicator is moved to the 0;00;04;21 position.

Figure 11-1

STEP 4 Select **Layer > Flatten Image** to convert the video clip into a single background image layer. Because you probably still need your original video file, select **Image > Duplicate** to create a duplicate copy of the still image. Then switch back to the original document and close the original video clip file without saving.

STEP 5 In the duplicate file, the image may look a bit jagged because it was captured from a motion video, which naturally has interlaced lines. To smooth out the image and replace the interlace lines, select **Filter > Video > De-Interlace**. When the De-interlace dialog box appears, select the elimination and create new fields options as desired. If you're not sure which options to select, choose Odd Fields and Interpolation. Figure 11-2 shows an example of an image before (left) and after (right) being de-interlaced. The change may be subtle, but it is necessary.

Figure 11-2

STEP 6 Apply any image correction techniques as needed, such as adjusting the Curves or Hue/Saturation, and make any other changes to the file for its final destination, such as modifying the size and resolution through the **Image > Image Size** menu. When you are satisfied with the quality of your new video still image, save the file in the desired format.

TECHNIQUE

12 USING THE PATTERN MAKER

TO BYPASS HAVING to create and offset your own pattern designs, another method for creating patterns involves using Photoshop's optional Pattern Maker plug-in. What's unique about this method is that the Pattern Maker allows you to quickly and easily create new patterns from extracted selections in other images. Your selections are then randomly sliced and reassembled into new patterns that can be used to fill any layer or selection. These custom patterns can also be easily saved as pattern presets to use with any of your other images in Photoshop. The only true drawback to this type of pattern is that it is virtually impossible to create a pattern that will tile seamlessly. On the other hand, if you're looking to create an irregular and chaotic pattern to lend a little grungy or weathered look to your existing images, this is the perfect technique.

INTERNET HINT: Before you can perform this technique, check your Filter menu to see if you have the Pattern Maker option. If not, you'll need to download and install the free Adobe Photoshop Pattern Maker plug-in:
Windows: http://www.adobe.com/support/downloads/detail.jsp?ftpID=4048
Mac OS: http://www.adobe.com/support/downloads/detail.jsp?ftpID=4047.

STEP 1   Open the image you want to use as the source for your pattern. Images with odd angles tend to work best. Because the Pattern Maker will convert the currently selected layer into the pattern layer, be sure to make a duplicate layer of your original image before you begin. To make the duplicate, drag the original layer to the Create a New Layer button at the bottom of the Layers panel.

STEP 2   Using any one of your Marquee tools, make a selection (or multiple selections) around any part(s) of your image and copy the selection to the Clipboard by pressing Ctrl+C/ ⌘+C.

STEP 3   Select **Filter** > **Pattern Maker** to open the Pattern Maker dialog box, as shown in Figure 12-1. On the right side of the screen, check the Use Clipboard as Sample checkbox to define the sampled area on your Clipboard for your pattern. Alternatively, you could use the Pattern Maker's Marquee tool to select a region within your image for the sample area. To create a pattern that will fill your entire document window, click the Use Image Size button; otherwise, enter values in the Width and Height fields to set the dimensions of your pattern's tile.

Figure 12-1

50

STEP 4   To create a pattern from your sampled region, click the Generate button. As shown in Figure 12-2, the newly created pattern will appear within the Pattern Maker dialog box as well as in the dialog box's Tile History preview area. To see another version of the tile, click the Generate Again button. You may click this button as many times as you like until you find a pattern that you like. Each new tile will be listed in the Tile History area. You may scroll through this section to review, delete, and save patterns.

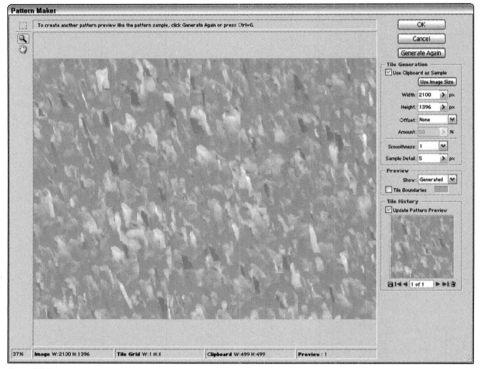

Figure 12-2

STEP 5   To use a pattern, you have two options, both of which will be performed here. First, to save the selected pattern tile as a pattern preset for future use, click the Saves Preset Pattern (floppy disc) icon in the Tile History section. When the Pattern Name dialog box appears, give your pattern a name and click OK. Your pattern is now saved as a preset and can be used as a pattern fill in any document at any time. Next, to use the pattern without having to apply the pattern preset to the currently selected layer, click OK.

STEP 6   To use your new patterned layer to useful effect, try adjusting the pattern layer's blending mode. For example, in the image shown in Figure 12-3, the pattern layer is set to Overlay.

51

Figure 12-3

To apply your new pattern preset to another file, open the desired image, click the Layers panel's Create New Fill or Adjustment Layer button, select Pattern, select your new pattern from the Pattern Fill dialog box, click OK, and if needed, modify the Adjustment Layer's blending mode. In the example in Figure 12-4, the same pattern fill was applied to the house using a layer mask and the blending mode set to Saturation, which gives the pattern a bit of a neon glow.

Figure 12-4

TECHNIQUE

13

DESIGNING A BLOG HEADER

AS YOU KNOW, blog headers come in a wide range of flavors and designs, and reflect all kinds of businesses and design aesthetics. Some headers are clean and simple using a limited range of line and color, others have that hand-drawn or organic vibe, some are truly awful and seem to have no semblance of color harmony or style, and still others have an elaborate and complicated look filled with overlapping patterns, layer effects, and styles. Ultimately, the look and feel of the design for your blog is up to you, but since this book is all about inspiration, your next blog header design should stand out from the crowd (in a good way). This chapter teaches you several tips to create a simple, yet visually compelling blog header design.

STEP 1   The size of your new document needs to match the size of your blog. Typical widths are 760 px and 960 px, but it can be any size within that range so long as the graphics match up with the underlying HTML/CSS/PHP structure. For this exercise, create a layout that is 955 px wide. Select **File > New** to open the New document dialog box. From Preset choose Web, which will automatically set the resolution to 72 px/inch and the color mode to RGB. Next, enter a width of 960, a height of 400, and click OK.

STEP 2   To set the background color of your layout, click on the foreground color swatch on the toolbar to open the Color Picker dialog box and enter the hex value **#b9ad8a** (or another color of your choice) at the bottom of the panel. Click OK to close the dialog box and then press Alt+Backspace/Option+Delete to fill your layout with the foreground color.

STEP 3   Within this space you'll create a patterned background for the header from a set of free Paisley Photoshop patterns created by Miriam Moshinsky of klukeart.com.

> INTERNET HINT: *For best results with this technique, use a pattern that you really, really like. For the ultimate collection of free Photoshop patterns, visit http://www.smashingmagazine.com/2009/02/12/the-ultimate-collection-of-free-photoshop-patterns/.*

But before you can do that, you need to create a new layer (Shift+Ctrl+N/Shift+⌘+N) called *Header BG*. Press the M key to select the Rectangular Marquee tool, and drag a 200 px tall rectangular selection across your layout that sits roughly 50 px from the top, as shown in Figure 13-1. If needed, use guides and the Info panel to help with sizing and positioning.

Figure 13-1

Next, press the D key to reset the foreground color to black and fill your selection with black by pressing Alt+Backspace/Option+Delete. Then press Ctrl+D/⌘+D to deselect the selection.

STEP 4   With the Header BG layer still selected, click the Add a Layer Style button at the bottom of the Layers panel and choose Pattern Overlay. When the Layer Style dialog box opens, click the Pattern menu to open the Pattern Picker and click on the pattern you want to use. To load a pattern from another source, select Load Patterns from the Pattern Picker options menu, navigate to and select the Patterns (*.PAT) file, and then click Load. When prompted to replace or append the existing patterns in the menu, choose Append. Your new patterns will be added to the bottom of the pattern picker and from there you can select your preferred pattern.

After you have selected your pattern, adjust the blending mode to Luminosity (which subtly desaturates the pattern) and modify the scale if needed. For instance, the scale of Paisley Pattern1 is set to 30%.

STEP 5   Still within the Layer Style dialog box, click on the Blending Options category and set the fill opacity of the advanced blending to 0%. This ensures that the pattern shows through but the black background color of the layer does not, allowing the pattern to take on the tint of the file's background color. Then, to add a bit of a vignette, select the Inner Glow category, adjust the blending mode to Linear Light, change the color to black, set the size to 100 px, and adjust the opacity to around 50%. Click OK to close the Layer Style dialog box. Your header should now look somewhat like Figure 13-2. Don't be afraid, however, to deviate from these steps; if you think a different blending mode looks better, by all means, use it!

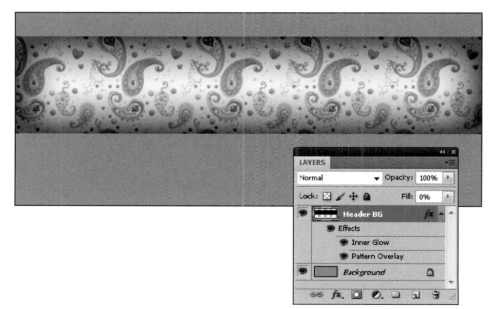

Figure 13-2

STEP 6   To make a separate area for the navigation, create a new layer (Shift+Ctrl+N/ Shift+⌘+N) called *Nav Bar*. Using the Rectangular Marquee, drag out a 50 px tall selection that sits below the Header BG layer, fill the selection with #7a5e21, and press Ctrl+D/⌘+D to deselect. Then press D to reset the foreground color to black.

As you did in Step 4, click the Add a Layer Style button at the bottom of the Layers panel and choose Pattern Overlay. This time, when the Layer Style dialog box opens, click the Pattern menu to open the Pattern Picker and select one of the Texture Fill patterns, such as Burlap. Adjust the blending mode to Color Burn (which subtly darkens and blends the pattern into the underlying background color) and modify the scale if needed.

Select the Gradient Overlay category and click the Gradient menu to select a black to transparent gradient (second gradient from the top left). Then adjust the opacity down to around 50%.

Select the stroke category and apply a 3 px outside stroke with the hex value of #b39540. Click OK to close the dialog box.

STEP 7   For symmetry, duplicate the *Nav Bar* layer by pressing Ctrl+J/⌘+J, rename it *Top Bar* in the Layers panel, and drag the new layer to the top part of your layout above the Header BG layer. Nice!

STEP 8   Next, to further define the header from the rest of your layout, you will add a shadow below the Nav Bar layer. To ensure that the layer is positioned in the correct order in the Layers panel, select the Header BG layer, press Shift+Ctrl+N/Shift+⌘+N, rename the new layer to *Shadow*, and then press the G key to select the Gradient tool. Before you drag out a shadow, select the foreground to transparent gradient (this should be second in the list showing as black to transparent) and the reflected gradient type from the Gradient Tool Options bar at the top of the workspace. Now, drag a short gradient about 30–40 px tall that spans downward past the bottom edge of the Nav Bar area.

For additional symmetry, duplicate the Shadow layer and move it in the layout so that it sits directly below the Top Bar layer. If needed, adjust the opacity of both shadow layers to soften the shadow effect.

STEP 9   Your header is nearly complete! The last step is to drop in the Logo/Logotype and navigation text. Save the file for later use in Technique #18, "Generating CSS Layers with Optimized Graphics." Figure 13-3 shows an example of the completed blog header.

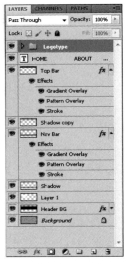

Figure 13-3

57

TECHNIQUE

14

CREATING DATA-DRIVEN GRAPHICS

IF YOU DO a lot of graphic production work as part of your job—whether that be for design, video, or print—you've probably wondered at some point whether there was a simple way to automate the process of creating multiple versions of a graphic. In fact, you may have even already read something about creating data-driven graphics, but then quickly gave up on the idea because it ultimately seemed too complicated a process to learn. Well, the time has come for renewed hope! Follow the steps in this technique to see how truly easy it is to generate multiple versions of the same graphic—each in its own PSD file—using different text and images from a single template design.

STEP 1 The first thing to do is to create a template file similar to the one shown in Figure 14-1. This template contains a total of six layers: an object (the car), text layer (car make and model), a label (classic car), the label's background, a tan border, and a white background.

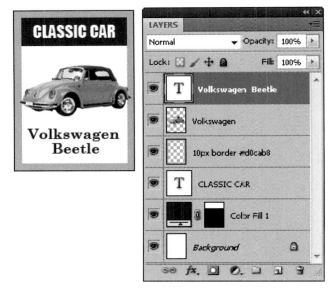

Figure 14-1

To create a similar template yourself, select **File > New** to open the New document dialog box. From Preset choose Web, set the width to 150, the height to 200, and click OK.

STEP 2 Press the U key to select the Rectangle tool and drag a rectangle that is 45 px tall across the top of the document. Click the Create New Fill or Adjustment Layer button at the bottom of the Layers panel and choose Solid Color. When the Color Picker dialog box opens, enter the hex value of **#342f2f** (dark brown ish gray) into the color field and click OK to close the dialog box.

STEP 3 Press the T key to select the Horizontal Type tool, and on the Type toolbar at the top of the screen, select Impact as the font, set the size to 20 pt, the color to white, and the alignment to center. Place your cursor on top of the gray rectangle and type the words **CLASSIC CAR**. Your type will appear on its own layer.

STEP 4 To add a 10 px tan stroke around the outer edges of the template, press Shift+Ctrl+N/Shift+⌘+N to create a new layer. Then press Ctrl+A/⌘+A to Select All and select **Edit > Stroke.** In the Stroke dialog box, set the width to 10 px, the color to #d0cab8, the location to inside, and click OK. Rename the layer *10 px border.*

STEP 5   Next, you add the car. Select **File** > **Place** to navigate to and open the first of your data-driven graphics into the template. When the placed image appears, resize as needed and press Enter/Return to accept the placed image into your file. Placed images become Smart Objects, which retain all of their original qualities, including scalability without loss of resolution.

STEP 6   Now you add a second layer of text. Press the T key to select the Horizontal Type tool. Set the font to Century Schoolbook Bold (or another serif style) as the font, set the size to 18 pt, set the leading to 18 pt, the color to black, and the alignment to center. Place your cursor between the car and the bottom of the layout and type (on two lines) the words **Volkswagen Beetle**. The template is now complete. Select **File** > **Save** and save the file onto your computer in the desired location.

STEP 7   Select **Image** > **Variables** > **Define** to open the Variables dialog box shown in Figure 14-2. With the Define option selected, use the Layer menu to choose the variable type for each layer in your file that you want to change within the template. For instance, the car layer should have the Pixel Replacement option selected and the car text layer should have the Text Replacement option selected. If you wanted to toggle on and off the visibility of another layer, select the Visibility option for that layer. Scroll through each layer in the dialog box and apply settings as needed. Do nothing for layers (such as the background) that will remain the same within each image to be generated from the template.

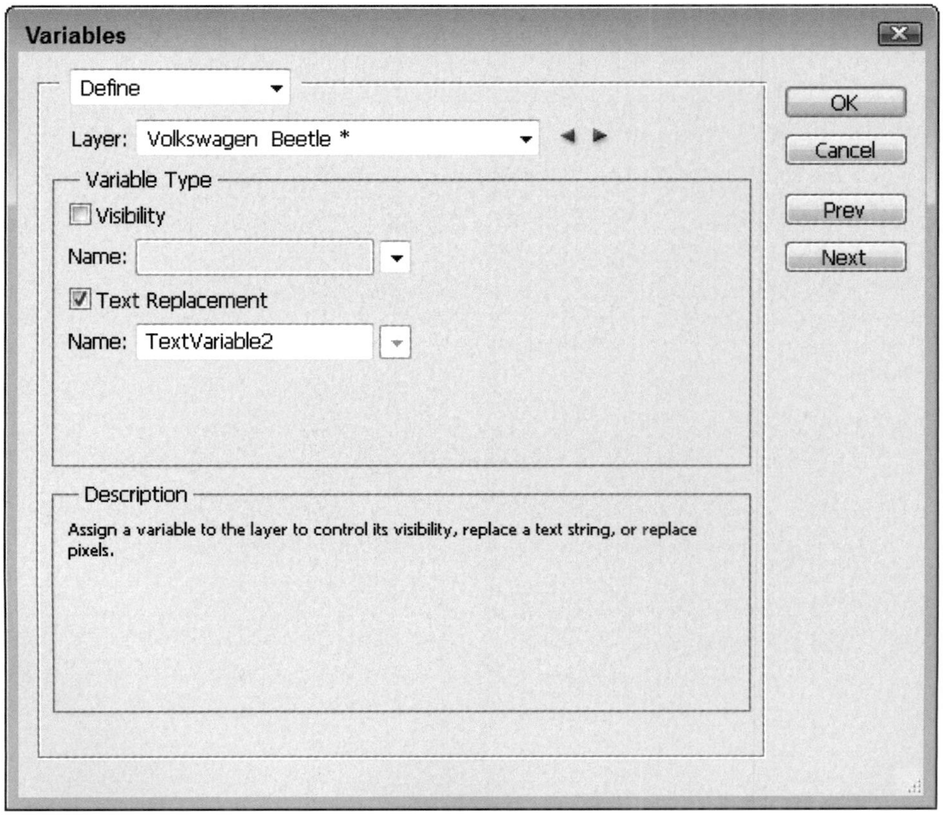

Figure 14-2

STEP 8   Click the Next button to view the Data Set options. Here you will define a data set for each version of the graphic you want to create; if you have 10 graphics, you will create 10 data sets.

You can import an existing data set text file or manually create individual data sets:

- To import a data set (such as a tab delimited text file), click the Import button and select the text file, set your import options and choose the encoding type for the file.
- To manually create your data sets, click the Create New Data Set button (looks like a floppy disk), choose a layer from the Name pop-up menu, and set the variable data for the selection. Layers can be visible or hidden, images can be replaced, and text can be changed. For example, Data Set 1 could use the exact images and text from the template, but Data Set 2 could use replacement images and text. When you have finished setting the variables for Data Set 1, click the Create New Data Set button to create variables for Data Set 2. Repeat this process to create additional data sets. When you're finished, click OK.

STEP 9   To generate graphics from your template, select **File > Export > Data Sets As Files**. In the Export dialog box that opens, click the Folder button to choose a destination for the generated graphics, choose the data sets to be exported (All Data Sets), provide a base name for the graphics (such as cars), and click OK. Within seconds, your new PDS files appear in the destination folder. Easy peasy. Figure 14-3 shows the three graphics generated from this template.

Figure 14-3

TECHNIQUE

15

BUILDING A SIMPLE WEB LAYOUT

WHEN IT COMES to building a Web layout, there are certain elements that need to be in place—how those elements look is totally up to you. The only real guiding principle you should keep in mind when making decisions about color, size, and arrangement is "less is more." The more breathing room you can give to the elements in your layout—the open space between design elements that designers refer to as *whitespace*—the easier it will be for visitors to take in what they see and easily move around the site. In this exercise, you will create a simple Web layout with limited colors, fonts, and styles for an overall look that is clean, open, and inviting.

STEP 1   Select **File > New** to open the New document dialog box. From Preset choose Web, set the width to 960, the height to 960, the background contents to white, and click OK. When the file opens, place a vertical guide at 10 px in from the left and another guide 10 px in from the right. These guides will serve as the margins of your layout.

Set the foreground color to #bde1ea, which will serve as your layout background color. Press the M key to select the Rectangular Marquee tool and drag a selection (940×960 px) between the guides. Press the Delete/Backspace key to open the Fill dialog box, select Foreground Color from the Use menu, and click OK.

STEP 2   To add a subtle gradient across the page, press Shift+Ctrl+N/Shift+⌘+N to create a new layer, set the foreground color to #2593af, and then press the G key to select the Gradient tool. On the Gradient control bar, make sure the gradient type is set to Foreground to Transparent and Linear Gradient. Then Shift+drag a gradient downwards across the document from the very top to about 700 px down.

STEP 3   Next you'll create the header. Leave your Foreground color set to #2593af, and set your background color to #136277. From the top of the page between the guides, drag another rectangle selection that is 940×166 px. Press Shift+Ctrl+N/Shift+⌘+N to create a new layer, and then press the G key to select the Gradient tool. On the Gradient control bar, set the gradient type to foreground to background and radial. Then, across the center of the selection, Shift+drag a horizontal gradient from the 200 px mark to the 800 px mark.

Drop in a logo, some text, a tagline, a phone number, and a 1 px white horizontal divider. Then add a text layer for the navigation. If desired, include an example of how the navigation over state will look when a visitor hovers over one of the nav buttons. Figure 15-1 shows an example of how the page might look so far.

STEP 4   To create a banner area 10 px below the header and roughly 10 px in from the guides, use the Rectangular Marquee to make a selection that is 921×188. Click the Create New Fill or Adjustment Layer button at the bottom of the Layers panel and choose Solid Color. When the Color Picker opens, enter the hex value of #**bde1ea** (light blue) into the color field and click OK to close the dialog box.

Click the Add a Layer Style button, apply a 10 px inside white stroke, and click OK to close the Layer Style dialog box. This banner area can be used for graphics, text, or any combination. If you'd like to make the banner interactive, add a simple text navigation system near the bottom-right edge. For this demonstration, you see a 23 px bold Arial header, 16 px Arial paragraph text, an icon, and a simple numerical navigation system (see Figure 15-2).

Figure 15-1

64

STEP 5   For the main content area of the layout, use the Rectangular Marquee selection and Solid Color adjustment layer technique to create a white rectangle roughly 920×466 px that sits about 10 px below the banner. Near the top of the white rectangle, add three evenly spaced headers in Arial bold 23 pt #136277 type, followed by three placeholder paragraphs using 14 pt Arial text, and three buttons that allow visitors to learn more about each topic.

> HINT: While final Web copy is always preferred in a mockup because it shows how the content actually looks within the layout, if you don't have access to the final copy while creating the design, feel free to use Greeking placeholder text (see, for example, www.lipsum.com) until the final copy becomes available.

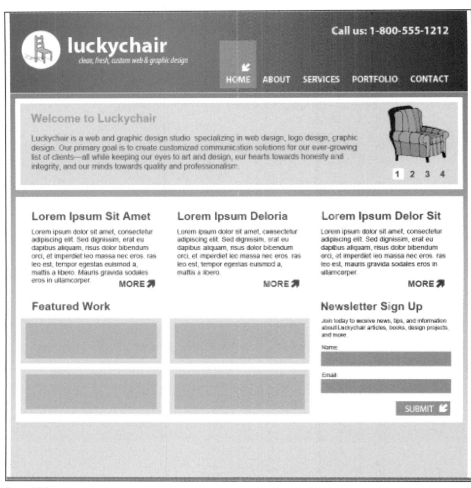

Figure 15-2

Below these three paragraphs, add two new headers, one for Featured Work and another for Newsletter Signup. Beneath the Featured Work header, use the Rectangle Shape tool to add four rectangular shapes inside which featured work will appear. Below the Newsletter header, add a few simple form elements, such as Name and Email fields and a Submit button. If desired, repeat any graphic elements you have used earlier in the layout to create a sense of visual consistency. In Figure 15-2, the arrow from the main navigation bar is repeated effectively in four places.

STEP 6   For the footer of the page, simply duplicate the header background layer and drag it to about 10 px below the main content area. Add some navigation links, a copyright notice, and some other content to fill the space, such as a list of recent blog posts.

For a final touch of dimensionality, add a drop shadow below both the banner and main content areas. Feel free to add other styles and elements to your layout to satisfy your personal design aesthetic. That's all there is to it! Figure 15-3 shows the final layout.

Figure 15-3

CREATING A LINED NOTEBOOK LAYOUT

ONE OF THE hardest things to do well on the Web is to create layouts that have some degree of dimensionality without looking too flat or too 3D. When you add too many graphics, however, you run the risk of having your pages load too slowly. One of the best workarounds, then, is to add some kind of texture or design element to the page without dramatically increasing the load time.

For example, nearly everyone uses lined notebook paper, so recreating the look of lined paper is a smart way to add a familiar element to your layout. In this exercise, you learn how to create lined notebook paper and use it effectively in a Web layout.

STEP 1   To create the lined notebook paper pattern you will use in this technique, select **File > New** to open the New document dialog box. Under Preset choose Web, set the width to 1, the height to 20, and click OK. Set the foreground color to #9fd7da, press the M key to select the Rectangular Marquee tool, select the 10th pixel from the top of the document, and press Delete/Backspace to fill the selection with the foreground color.

To define the pattern, press Ctrl+A/⌘+A to select all, and then select **Edit > Define Pattern**. When the Pattern Name dialog box appears, name your pattern *Lined Notebook* and click OK. Save and close the pattern file.

STEP 2   For the layout document, select **File > New** to open the New document dialog box. From Preset choose Web, set the width to 960, the height to 960, the background contents to white, and click OK. When the file opens, place a vertical guide at 10 px in from the left and another guide 10 px in from the right. These guides will serve as the margins of your layout.

Next, press the M key to select the Rectangular Marquee tool and drag a selection (942×960 px) between the guides. Click the Create New Fill or Adjustment Layer button at the bottom of the Layers panel and choose Pattern. When the Pattern dialog box opens, your new lined notebook pattern should fill the selection. If not, click the pattern menu button, scroll down to the bottom of the pattern listing, and select your new pattern. Click OK to close the dialog box.

STEP 3   Set the foreground color to #fba2aa and, using the Line tool roughly 32 px in from the left edge, Shift+drag from the top to the bottom of the layout to insert a 1 px wide vertical "margin" line.

Next, you'll add all the header graphics. In the top 160 px of the layout, insert a logo, company name, tagline, phone number, search box, and navigation bar. If desired, add an example of how the navigation over state will look when a visitor hovers over one of the nav buttons. Because this example will be for a school-supply Website, the layout uses Eraser and Squeeky Chalk Sound chalk fonts and the KidTYPEPaint handwriting font to give the design a hand-written feel. Figure 16-1 shows an example of the page so far.

> *INTERNET HINT: For free chalk and handwriting style fonts, check out http://www.fontspace.com and http://www.1001fonts.com.*

STEP 4   To create an area for weekly specials that looks like a chalkboard, use the Rectangular Marquee to make a 940×214 px selection. Click the Create New Fill or Adjustment Layer button at the bottom of the Layers panel and choose Solid Color. When the Color Picker opens, enter the hex value of **#272f31** (dark gray) into the color field and click OK to close the dialog box.

Figure 16-1

Click the Add a Layer Style button at the bottom of the Layers panel, select Stroke, and apply a 15 px inside stroke, but instead of filling it with a solid color, choose Pattern from the Fill Type menu and select the Rusted Metal pattern from the Patterns menu. If the Rusted Metal pattern isn't showing, click the Pattern pop-up menu, load the Pattern library named Patterns, and select Rusted Metal.

Next, select the Bevel and Emboss style and add a 3 px, smooth, inner bevel. Click OK to close the Layer Style dialog box.

Using a chalkboard font, add the words **Back to School Specials** along the left side of the chalkboard and slightly rotate it counter-clockwise using the **Transform > Rotate** command. To the right of this, add three sale items with labels and promotional text. Take a look at Figure 16-2 for inspiration.

STEP 5   For the main content area of the page, break up the layout into three equal columns and fill each with a header, paragraph text, and Add To Cart button, followed by a product category header and product box (which you can replace later with product images). In this layout, the headers are Arial bold, the paragraph text is Arial regular, the buttons use Arial bold, and the boxes were made with the Rectangle tool.

The final touch is adding a footer navigation bar, which includes text links, copyright information, phone number, and links to additional customer support pages. The completed layout is shown in Figure 16-3.

Figure 16-2

Figure 16-3

OPTIMIZING TO SIZE

WHEN YOU'RE CREATING graphics for the Web, one of the main concerns is how to retain quality at a lower resolution. Whereas graphics meant for print have a 300 ppi, Web graphics typically only need 72 ppi. In addition to creating compelling images, banners, and Websites, Web designers are also often tasked with ensuring that the file size of these optimized graphics falls within a specified range. For example, the IAB (iab.net) recommends that a 300×250 px Medium Rectangle banner ad has a maximum initial download file weight of 40 KB or less. Even so, your particular project may have even tighter file size requirements, such as a banner that must be 10 KB or less.

In this chapter, you will learn a simple trick called Optimize to Size, which allows you to optimize your Web graphics in the desired file format of your choice at—or below—your targeted file size.

STEP 1   For demonstration purposes, you can use a simple banner ad like the one in Figure 17-1. If you don't have a graphic to practice this technique with, open up any file you have handy or mock something up quickly that looks like the example shown here.

Figure 17-1

STEP 2   Select **File > Save for Web & Devices** to open the Save For Web & Devices dialog box. For this practice image, the GIF or PNG-8 file format is most appropriate since the image contains large flat areas of color, no gradients, and no photographs. Therefore, from the Preset menu, select GIF 128 No Dither. Notice the file size displaying in the bottom-left corner of the preview pane. For this image, the file size with these optimization settings is 11KB. If you needed to ensure that the file was 10KB or less, you could adjust the various optimization settings until you get the file size where you need it to be. But to speed things along, there's a better way.

STEP 3   Click the Options menu in the top-right corner of the dialog box (to the right of the Preset menu) and select Optimize to File Size. In the dialog box that opens, set the desired file size to 10, set the Start With to Current Settings, and set the Use to Current Slice. Then click OK. Figure 17-2 shows the location of the options menu and Optimize to Size dialog box.

Photoshop automatically adjusts the optimization settings for you, giving you an image that has the maximum quality that meets or is less than your target size! Click Save to save a copy of the optimized graphic.

Options menu

Figure 17-2

TECHNIQUE 18

GENERATING CSS LAYERS WITH OPTIMIZED GRAPHICS

EACH TIME YOU optimize a sliced graphic layout in Photoshop, the default settings when you choose the HTML and Images Format in the Save Optimized As dialog box are set to export your graphics inside an HTML formatted table. Although it might be helpful, a tables-based layout isn't always the most practical or accessible way to code an HTML page. The best method for laying out pages is to use CSS layers. Layers are more flexible and forgiving than tables, and their position, style, and contents call all be controlled by CSS.

To force Photoshop to generate CSS when you output your sliced graphic layout with HTML and Images, follow the steps in this technique.

STEP 1   First, you will need a simple layout that you can carve into four slices, such as the blog header layout you created in Technique #13, "Designing a Blog Header." If you have that file handy, open it in Photoshop. Otherwise, create a quick layout similar to the one in Figure 13-3 before you proceed.

Press Ctrl+R/⌘+R to turn on your rulers and drag three guides onto the document to separate the different sections of the layout, as shown in Figure 18-1.

Figure 18-1

STEP 2   Press the C key to select the Crop tool, and then press Shift+C to toggle to the Slice tool hidden below it. On the Slice tool's options bar, click the Slices From Guides button and Photoshop will create slices from the guides. Now the file is ready for optimization.

STEP 3   Select **File > Save for Web & Devices** to open the Save For Web & Devices dialog box so you can set the optimization rules for each slice. Using the Slice tool, Shift+click to select slices 1, 3, and 4 and choose PNG-8 128 Dithered from the Preset menu. Now click to select slice 2 and choose JPEG High from the Preset menu.

STEP 4   Click the Save button to launch the Save Optimized As dialog box. Navigate to the location on your computer you would like to save the files into. Then enter a base name for your files in the File Name field, select HTML and Images from the Format menu, select All Slices from the Slices menu, and from the Settings menu, select Other to open the Output Settings dialog box. Click the Next button until you see the Slices options, as shown in Figure 18-2. Select the Generate CSS option in the Slice Output area and click the Referenced menu to choose how you would like the layers referenced, either inline, By ID, or By Class. If you're unsure which one to choose, pick By ID.

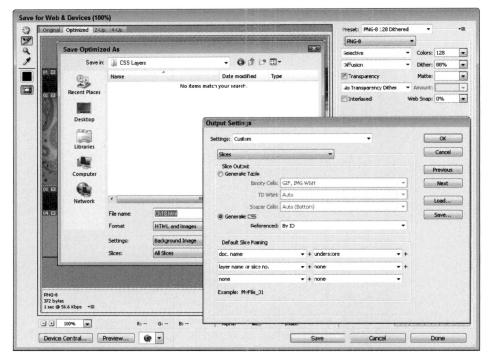

Figure 18-2

Click the Next button again until you see HTML options and click the Output XHTML option. This will ensure that the output HTML code follows XHTML coding specifications, which will make your pages accessible to the widest possible audience. Click OK to close the dialog box with these settings, and click Save to save the images in an HTML file using CSS layers.

STEP 5   To preview your HTML page in a browser, double-click the HTML file icon or drag and drop the icon into an open browser window. You can check the source code to see your layers and CSS styles by selecting View Source from the browser's Edit menu. To make further edits to the page, open the HTML file in your preferred HTML/WYSIWYG editor.

TECHNIQUE 19

EXPORTING LARGE IMAGES TO ZOOMIFY™

SO, YOU HAVE some amazing high-resolution photographs that you want to show on your Website, but you know the second you adjust the resolution down to 72 ppi that the images simply won't be that impressive. Of course, you could throw the images into a Flash movie and then stick the movie on the page, but that would take extra time and resources that you don't really have or want to use. So what should you do?

Zoomify™, baby! This hot little Flash-based viewer has been around since CS3, but hardly anyone knows about it because of *where* the tool is in Photoshop. Follow the instructions here to learn how you can add "pan and zoomable" high-resolution images to your Web pages with no loss of quality or added file weight—all with one simple click.

STEP 1   Start by opening a high-resolution image into Photoshop, such as this shot of the Manhattan skyline through Central Park, taken from the roof of the Metropolitan Museum of Art (see Figure 19-1). Typical high-res images will be 300 dpi in the TIFF, PDF, JPG, or PSD format.

Figure 19-1

STEP 2   Select **File > Export > Zoomify** to open the Zoomify™ Export dialog box, shown in Figure 19-2.

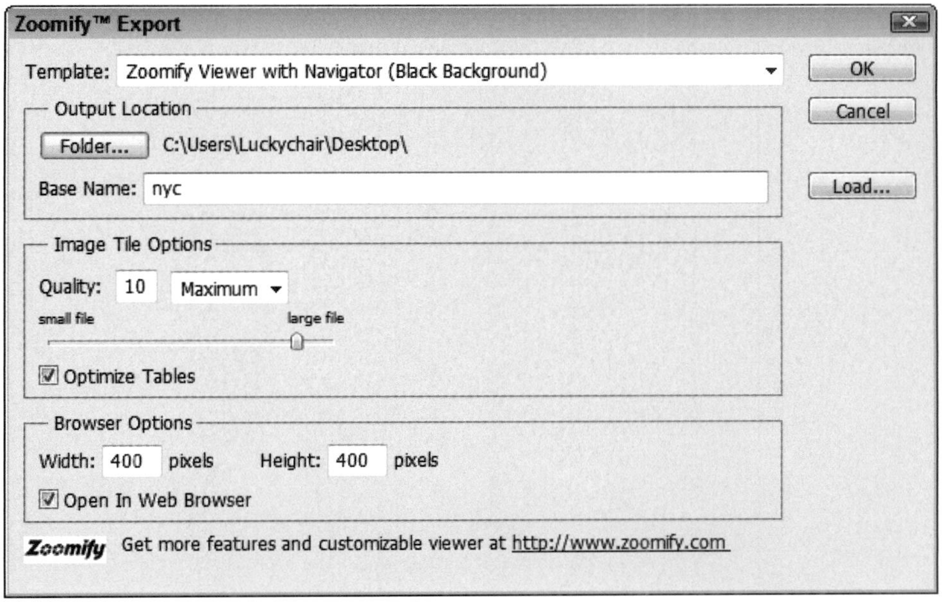

Figure 19-2

STEP 3 The first thing to do is select a Zoomify™ viewer template from the Template menu. The default viewer is set to Zoomify Viewer (Black Background), but you can also choose a white or gray background either with or without the Navigator.

STEP 4 Click the Folder button to select the output location on your local computer. Enter a Base Name for the image, such as *centralpark* or *nyc*.

> HINT: To ensure Zoomify™ outputs your image with XHTML valid code, use only lowercase letters for the base name and avoid using special characters (such as ñ or é) and punctuation (such as periods or slashes).

STEP 5 In the Image Tile Options area, set the quality for your image between 0 and 12. The higher the number is, the better the quality and the bigger the file output. Amazingly, even at the highest setting, Zoomify™ only adds about 20 KB to your page for each image. Leave the Optimize Tables option checked for best compression quality.

STEP 6 To set the size of your base image within the Zoomify™ viewer, enter a pixel width and height in the Browser Options area. To view your finished image in a browser, leave the Open In Web Browser option checked.

STEP 7   Click OK to close the dialog box. Photoshop will export your image to your output location as an HTML file, along with a folder full of all the tile images that make up the larger high-resolution image that displays within the Zoomify™ browser viewer. If you left the Open In Web Browser option checked, your new page will also open in a local browser window, like the example shown in Figure 19-3. When you're finished using the Zoomify™ Export tool, you can upload both the HTML file and images folder to your live Web server.

Figure 19-3

INTERNET HINT: For added viewer features, product support, or to purchase a fully customizable viewer for under $30 US, visit http://www.zoomify.com. To watch a video on using Zoomify™, visit http://www.adobe.com/go/vid0003.

IMAGE PROCESSING TO RESIZE AND OPTIMIZE

ONE OF THE not-so-exciting parts of being a designer is getting to perform repetitive tasks such as resizing and optimizing a bunch of images. Whether you're working on a dozen or 100 or more files at a time, with Photoshop you don't need to sludge through the same set of tasks for each image. Follow the steps here to learn how to run the Image Processor on selected open files or the contents of a specified folder.

STEP 1 Select **File > Scripts > Image Processor** to open the Image Processor dialog box, shown in Figure 20-1, which is divided into four sections.

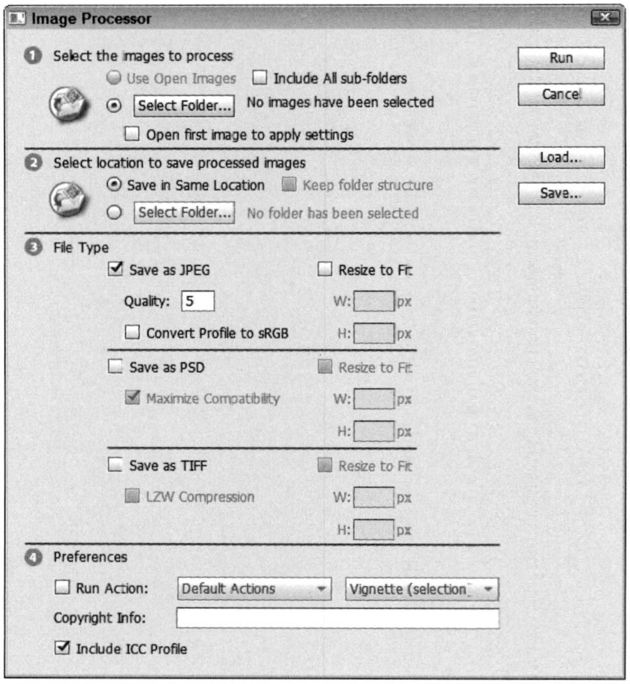

Figure 20-1

STEP 2 In the first section, choose the source location of the images you want to process. This can be either all the images open in your workspace or a specific folder that you select by clicking the Select Folder button. When selecting a folder you can also choose to include sub-folders and/or have Camera Raw open for the first image so that you can apply specific settings that will be used on the remaining images.

In the second section, click the Select Folder button to set the destination location of your processed files, which can either be the same location as the source or another specified folder.

STEP 3 For the File Type in the third section, select the desired output file format. Choose JPEG, PSD, or TIFF, as well as Width and Height file dimensions in pixels if you want to resize the output images. For example, you may want to convert a folder's worth of high-resolution photographs into low-resolution JPEGs with a max width and max height of 450 px. Be sure to enter values for both dimensions.

> HINT: To save the file as a Photoshop PDF, select Run Action in section 4 and choose the Save as Photoshop PDF Action from the Default Actions set.

STEP 4   The Preferences settings in the fourth section are totally optional:

- To apply a Photoshop action, check the Run Action box and choose an Action Set and Action from the menus.
- To include copyright metadata with your images, enter text into the Copyright Info field.
- To include an ICC Profile, check the Include ICC Profile box.

STEP 5   When you have finished configuring all the settings, click the Run button. Photoshop will automatically open, process, close, and save your new images in the target location.

> *INTERNET HINT: To download an ultimate collection of useful Photoshop actions, visit http://www.smashingmagazine.com/2008/10/20/the-ultimate-collection-of-useful-photoshop-actions/.*

84

TECHNIQUE

21

CREATING FRAME-BASED GIF ANIMATIONS

BEFORE FLASH CAME around, back in the mid 1990s, most designers added movement to a Web page by creating simple frames-based animated GIFs. Frames animation allows you to create the illusion of movement by displaying a series of image frames in a single file, each for a specified number of seconds, much like Eadweard Muybridge's series of high-speed stop-motion photographs might have appeared when viewed through his invented motion projector, the Zoopraxiscope, back in the late 1870s.

Despite Flash's continued popularity, animated GIFs are still a great file format for advertising banners, logos, and icons (including favicons). Read this technique to learn how to create your own frames-based animated GIF files using Photoshop's Animation panel.

STEP 1   To perform the steps in this technique, you will need a Photoshop file with a series of 10 images placed on 10 separate layers, with only the first layer visible, like the example of Muybridge's human motion study shown in Figure 21-1.

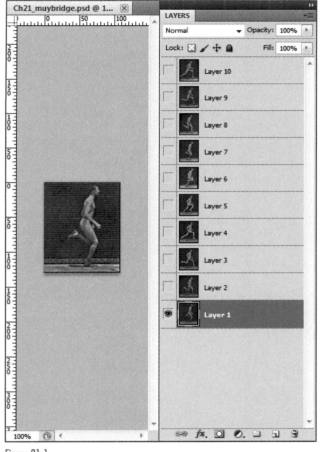

Figure 21-1

STEP 2   Select **Window > Animation** to open the Animation panel. The panel opens up in Timeline view by default, so to switch over to Frames view, click the Convert to Frame Animation button in the panel's lower-right corner. In Frames view, you will see one frame in the panel that displays a thumbnail of the selected layer visible in the Layers panel.

STEP 3   From the Animation panel's options menu at the top-right corner of the Animation panel, click the Make Frames From Layers options and Photoshop will do just that. Your Animation panel should now be populated with a total of 10 frames, one frame per layer, as illustrated in Figure 21-2.

Figure 21-2

STEP 4   With Frame 1 selected, Shift+click on Frame 10 to select all 10 frames (or choose Select All Frames from the panel's options menu). On the first frame, click the Frame Delay Time menu next to where it says 0 sec to set the delay to 0.1 seconds. Then click the Looping Options menu next to where it says Once and choose Forever. These settings will be applied to all selected frames.

STEP 5   Now comes the fun part. To preview your animation, click the Play button below the frames, and to stop the preview, press Stop. Cool! One thing, though, is that your animation might be playing backwards due to the position of the layers in the Layers panel. To flip the order of the frames, select Reverse Frames from the panel's options menu.

STEP 6   Select **File > Save for Web & Devices** to save your animated GIF. When the dialog box opens, choose GIF 128 No Dither from the Preset menu and adjust the other optimization settings as needed. Then click the Save button to save the file on your computer.

If you'd like to test the animated GIF in a browser before adding it to your Web page, drag and drop the file by its icon into an open browser window. If you can't see the animation playing in your browser, upgrade your browser and check to see that the file has the .gif extension before trying again.

87

TECHNIQUE

22

BUILDING TIMELINE-BASED ANIMATED GIF BANNER ADS

WHILE PHOTOSHOP EXTENDED is not an animation program by any means, you can use it to create simple animations that include changes in your layer's position, opacity, and style using the Animation panel's Timeline view.

In this technique, you will discover how to build a timeline-based animated GIF file in Photoshop Extended's Animation panel.

STEP 1 This technique will work best if you start with a Photoshop file that includes a background, foreground object, some text, and a button, like the example in Figure 22-1. You're going to make the car move into the frame from the left to the center, and then flash the button off and on one time before the animation stops. For best results, organize your layers into folders so that you can easily manage each item in the animation.

Figure 22-1

STEP 2 Select **Window > Animation** to open the Animation panel. If the panel opens up in Frames view, click the Convert to Timeline Animation button in the panel's lower-right corner. In Timeline view, you will see each folder and layer of your file represented as a layer on the left of the timeline stage.

Adjust the visibility and position the objects on each layer to match your desired animation starting position. For example, to make the car drive in from the left, move the car layer to the left of the document window so that only the nose of the car sticks slightly into the frame, as illustrated in Figure 22-2.

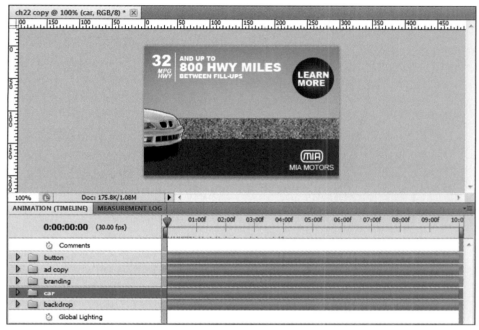

Figure 22-2

STEP 3 With the Current Time Indicator at the first frame, expand the timeline's car layer and click the stopwatch icon next to the word "Position" to set the first keyframe for this layer. If desired, the starting keyframe can be placed at different position along the timeline. You can also set keyframes for other layer properties at the same time.

STEP 4 To make it appear like the car is moving into the frame, move the blue Current Time Indicator in the Animation panel to the right along the timeline to about the 06:00 spot where you want the next keyframe to go, and then change the layer property. In this case, that means dragging the Car layer to its new position, which automatically inserts a new keyframe.

Changes to layer properties include moving the position of a layer, changing a layer's opacity, changing the position of a layer mask, or tuning a layer mask on or off.

STEP 5 Now for the button: Leaving the Current Time Indicator where it is at the 06:00 position, expand the Button layer in the Animation panel and on the button's shape layer, click the stopwatch icon next to the word "Opacity" to set the first keyframe for this layer.

Move the Current Time Indicator to 06:30 and adjust the opacity of the Button layer to 0% in the Layers panel. This will put a new keyframe at the 06:30 time mark. Now move the Current Time Indicator to 07:00 and adjust the opacity of the Button layer back to 100%. You should now have two keyframes for the car movement and three keyframes on the button's shape layer, as illustrated in Figure 22-3.

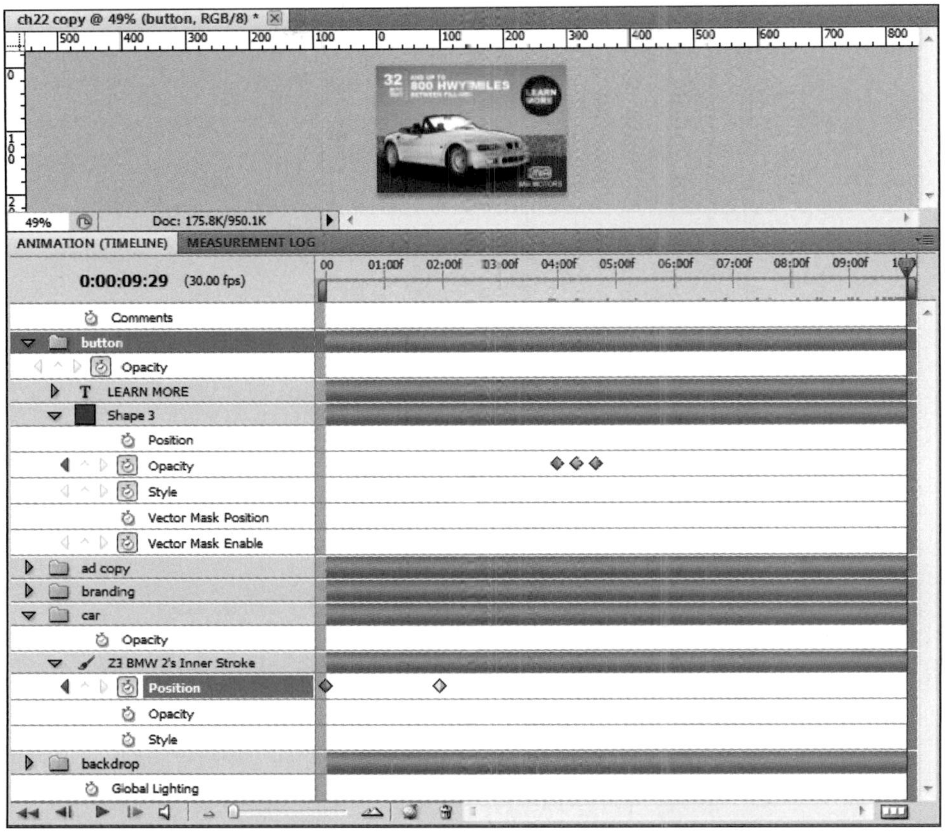

Figure 22-3

STEP 6 To preview your animation, drag the Current Time Indicator back to 00 and click the Play button. To stop the preview, press Stop. To adjust the movie's time and frame rate, select Document Settings from the panel's options menu on the top-right corner of the panel.

STEP 7 Select **File > Save for Web & Devices** to save your animated GIF. When the dialog box opens, choose GIF 128 Dithered from the Preset menu and adjust the other optimization settings as needed. To pull the best quality out of this image, adjust the colors to 256. If you'd like to change the number of times the animation will play, make a selection from the Looping Options menu. Otherwise, click the Save button to save the file as an animated GIF on your computer.

> HINT: If you'd like to test the animated GIF in a browser before adding it to your Web page, drag and drop the file by its icon into an open browser window. If you can't see the animation playing in the browser, upgrade your browser to the latest version and check to see that your file has the .gif extension before trying again.

91

DESIGNING CSS BUTTONS

WHEN IT COMES to making buttons on the Web, your primary goal is to design good-looking buttons that visitors will actually click to access the different products and services available on a site. Lately, the trend is to design big, colorful chunky buttons with easily readable text and clearly defined normal (or idle) and over states.

As for how the buttons function, you could use JavaScript to create a rollover button from two identically sized button graphics. But, the cleaner, more efficient way to do it is to create a single button graphic that contains both button states and then control the visibility of the button's parts using CSS. That is the topic of this chapter.

STEP 1 Select **File > New** to open the New document dialog box. Under Preset choose Web, set the Width to 200, the Height to 100, and click OK. Press Ctrl+R/⌘+R to turn on the Rulers, and then drag a horizontal guide from the top ruler to the 50 px line and drag out four more guides to sit along the outer edges of the file as shown in Figure 23-1.

STEP 2 Press U and Shift+U to select the Rounded Rectangle tool and set the Radius to 10 px on the tool's Options bar at the top of the screen. Using the guides to help, drag a rectangle shape across the top half of the file. Double-click the layer's color thumbnail in the Layers panel and set the color to #6faa35 (leafy green).

Figure 23-1

STEP 3 That's a nice button shape, but it's flat and dull. Click the Add a Layer Style button at the bottom of the Layers panel and add the following styles and settings:

- **Inner Shadow:** Set the blending mode to Multiply, the color to #78b52a (a lighter green), the opacity to 75%, the angle to 120°, and the distance and size to 5 px each.
- **Gradient Overlay:** Click the Gradient bar to edit the gradient. Set the left color to #406313 and the right color to #8fc41c, and click OK.
- **Stroke:** Set the size to 1 px, the position to inside, the fill type to Color, and the color to #36540d.

Click OK to close the Layer Style dialog box.

STEP 4 You're almost there. Set the Foreground color on the toolbar to #dff0ba and press Shift+Ctrl+N/Shift+⌘+N to create a new layer. Press G to select the Gradient tool and select the Foreground to Transparent gradient and the Radial Gradient type from the Gradient tool's Options bar at the top of the workspace. Now, drag a short gradient about 25 px tall that spans downward from the top-center edge of the button to the middle. This lightens the center of the button just a hint, providing a subtle yet effective amount of added dimensionality.

STEP 5   Press T to select the Horizontal Type tool, set your font to Arial Rounded MT, bold (or something similar), 23 pt, and White, and type the words **ADD TO CART** in the center of the green button. Then click the Add a Layer Style button and add a drop shadow with the blending mode set to Multiply, the color set to #283e07, and the distance and size both set to 1 px. Fabulous! This takes care of the button's normal state.

STEP 6   To create the button's over state, select the button, radial gradient, and text layers in the Layers panel, select Duplicate Layers from the panel's Options menu, and use the Move tool to move all three new layers to the bottom half of the document window.

Double-click the bottom button's Layer Style icon to open the Layer Style dialog box so you can adjust the button's Gradient Overlay settings. Click the Gradient bar to edit the gradient, set the left color to #3a0658, the right color to #d01557, and click OK. Click OK again to close the Layer Style dialog box. Your file should now look like the example in Figure 23-2.

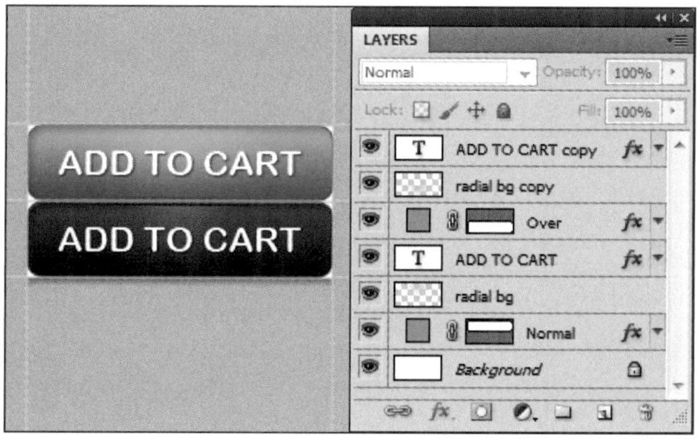

Figure 23-2

STEP 7   Optimize your graphic as a GIF or PNG using the Save For Web & Devices dialog box, and when you're ready to add the image to your page, be sure to add the following code highlighted in bold to your file and CSS:

```
<!DOCTYPE html PUBLIC "-//W3C//DTD XHTML 1.0 Transitional//EN"
"http://www.w3.org/TR/xhtml1/DTD/xhtml1-transitional.dtd">
<html xmlns="http://www.w3.org/1999/xhtml">
<head>
<meta http-equiv="Content-Type" content="text/html; charset=utf-8" />
<title>Untitled Document</title>
<style type="text/css">
<!--
.mybutton {
    width:200px;
    height:50px;
    display:block;
    text-indent:-9999px;
}
```

94

```css
.mybutton a {
    width:100%;
    height:100%;
    display:block;
    background-color: transparent;
    background-image: url(addtocart.png);
    background-repeat: no-repeat;
    background-position: left top;
}
.mybutton a:hover {
    background-position:0 -50px;
}
-->
</style>
</head>
<body>
<p class="mybutton"><a href="#">ADD TO CART</a></p>
</body>
</html>
```

PHOTOSHOP CS4 AND CS5 TECHNIQUES

TECHNIQUE

24

EDITING WITH ADJUSTMENT LAYER MASKS

LET'S FACE IT. Even when armed with the best camera and lighting equipment, you don't always produce the best, well-exposed photographs for every given lighting situation. Furthermore, you can't always guarantee the quality of the images you are given to work with for any particular project. Many times, you start out with a nice image that simply has a few exposure issues in key areas.

Now, presumably you know that non-destructive editing (**Layer > New Adjustment Layer**) is better than destructive editing (Image > Adjustments). But, did you know that you can create non-destructive layer masks to edit and refine parts of your images? Read on to learn more.

STEP 1   Start by opening an image in your workspace that has some areas of underexposure, like the theme park image shown in Figure 24-1.

The first thing you'll notice is that it's a cloudy day, which unevenly lights the subject. The foreground seems underexposed, the background could use a little vibrance, and the middle ground needs some sharpening. The image could also benefit from some additional lighting or a lens flare to place emphasis on the scene's focal point, the Ferris wheel in the center of the image.

Figure 24-1

STEP 2   Select **Layer > New Adjustment Layer > Curves** to add a Curves Adjustment layer. When the New Layer dialog box appears, change the Mode to Screen and click OK.

In the Adjustments panel, use the Black Point and White Point markers (they look like eyedroppers) to select white and black points within your image to improve overall tonality. Then click in the center of the diagonal curves adjustment line to set the gray point for the image and then drag it into a position that improves the exposure for the image foreground. For example, with the Ferris wheel scene, the exposure for this image improves when the gray point moves to the top of the middle peak of the tonal range, as seen in Figure 24-2.

STEP 3   The foreground does look better now, but the background and sky areas look completely blown out. To correct these areas, you're going to modify the Curves layer mask.

Click on the mask thumbnail on the Curves layer to select it. By default, the mask is completely white because it is revealing the adjustment across the entire image. Press X to swap the foreground and background colors so that black is on top. Press B to select the Paintbrush tool. In the Options bar, select a large soft-edged brush around 800 px and set the opacity to 70%. Then paint across the sky and upper edges of the theme park to conceal those parts of the scene from the Curves adjustment layer.

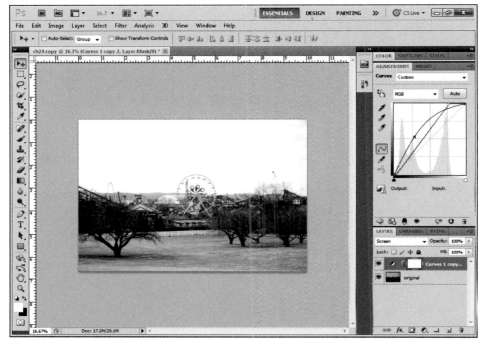

Figure 24-2

STEP 4   Now the foreground looks good, but the sky seems dark and gloomy. To correct the sky, you will create a new Curves adjustment layer that uses the reverse of the current Curves layer mask. With the Curves layer still selected, press Ctrl+J/⌘+J to duplicate the layer, switch over to the Masks panel (you'll find the Masks tab right next to the Adjustments tab in the Panel dock), and then click the Invert button on the Masks panel. The sky still looks washed out, but that's because you're still seeing the first Curves layer adjustment in full force. To edit the second Curves layer curve, open the Adjustments panel and move the position of the gray point along the curve to a place where the sky has depth and character. Much better, but the image can still use some improvements.

101

STEP 5   Ultimately, you want a crisp, clear, balanced image that contains one or more focal points or areas of interest. You can accomplish this in a few different ways, depending on your specific image. Try one or more of the following to get results similar to Figure 24-3:

- Click the Brightness/Contrast icon on the Adjustments panel to apply a Brightness/Contrast Adjustment layer.
- Click the Hue/Saturation icon on the Adjustments panel to apply a Hue/Saturation Adjustment layer.
- Convert your main image into a Smart Object (select the layer and choose Convert to Smart Object from the layer's context menu) and apply the Sharpening filter (**Filter > Sharpen > Smart Sharpen**).
- Convert your main image into a Smart Object and apply Lens Flare to the focal point using the Lens Flare filter (**Filter > Render > Lens Flare**).

Figure 24-3

HINT: If you're working with Photoshop CS4 or earlier, use the Create New Fill or Adjustment Layer button at the bottom of the Layers panel to add the Brightness/ Contrast and Hue/Saturation adjustment layers.

TECHNIQUE

25

USING CONTENT-AWARE SCALING

FINDING THE RIGHT picture for the job is no easy task. You know what that's like; you have the perfect idea in your mind, completely realized, and just need to find the right photograph to fit that layout. In the best-case scenario, you have the tools and resources to commission a photograph that meets your specifications. At other times, however, you must rely on stock art, seeking out an image that most closely matches your ideal, even if it comes up somewhat short. And by short, that can often mean that the image is good, but its orientation or dimensions are lacking in some way. It's either too wide, too narrow, too tall, too short, or the elements within it aren't quite spaced the way you wished they were.

Now, thanks to *content-aware scaling*, you can easily transform your images to fit within your layout—all without distorting the overall integrity of the original image file.

STEP 1   Begin by opening a Photoshop layout in your workspace. The layout can be for print, Web, or video, so long as it contains a space for adding an image that doesn't quite fit the space. For example, Figure 25-1 shows a Website layout with an area for a banner image across the top. The layout includes an image that would work, but it's not quite wide enough for the space it needs to fit into.

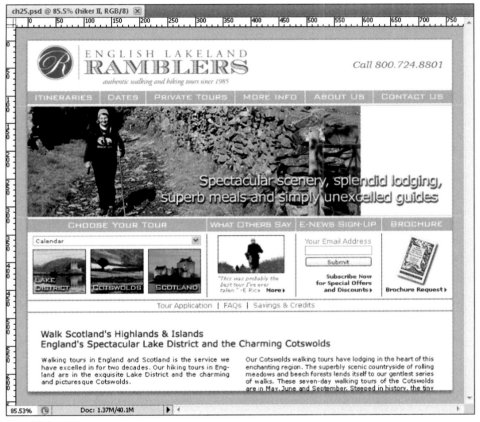

Figure 25-1

STEP 2   The example image shows a woman hiking along a trail. With a regular transformation, her figure would be stretched unnaturally and become pixilated as the image was scaled horizontally. The better solution is to use content-aware scaling, which will only stretch particular pixels within the file, retaining a more natural-looking final image after scaling.

Before you do that, however, you may want to protect certain parts of the file. Press W to select the Quick Selection tool (or feel free to use any of the other selection tools) and with your image layer selected, create a selection for the areas within your image that you want to remain static during the content-aware scale. If desired, click the Refine Edge button to apply a slight feather along the edges. Choose **Select > Save Selection** to save the selection, and when the Save Selection dialog box opens, name your selection and click OK. Press Ctrl+D/ ⌘+D to deselect.

STEP 3   Choose **Edit > Content-Aware Scale**. As with a normal transformation, your image appears with a bounding box ready for scaling, however with a content-aware scale, you can make certain refinements on the Options bar at the top of the screen. Under the Protect menu, choose the name of your saved selection, and to the right of that menu, click the Protect Skin Tones icon. Now you can scale the image horizontally to fill the space. Notice how the picture widens but the hiker within the protected selection area stays perfectly proportioned! So you can see how well this works, Figure 25-2 shows how the image would look when scaled normally and Figure 25-3 shows the final result with Content-Aware Scaling. Pretty amazing, eh?

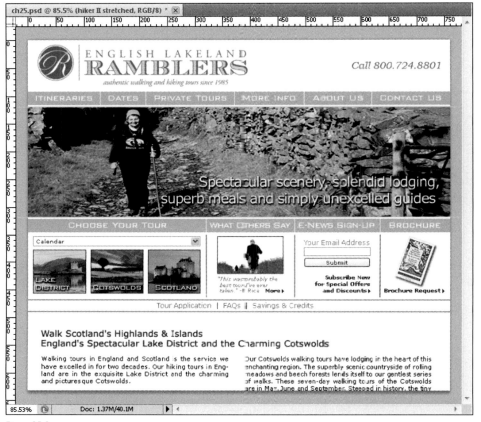

Figure 25-2

Figure 25-3

TECHNIQUE

26

CORRECTING IMAGE DISTORTION

IF YOU HAVE an 8- or 16-bit digital photograph that contains any of the more common lens flaws, such as unwanted *vignetting* (darkened corners), *pincushion* and *barrel distortion* (puckered or bloated in the center), and *chromatic aberration* (fuzzy color fringes outlining objects within the image), don't despair; use the super-simple Photoshop Lens Correction Filter to correct them.

STEP 1   Open an image in your workspace that contains some kind of lens flaw or perspective issue. For instance, the image in Figure 26-1 has a sign pole that, due to lens distortion, appears to be tilting backward.

Figure 26-1

STEP 2   Choose **Filter > Lens Correction** (in CS4, choose **Filter > Distort > Lens Correction**) to open the Lens Correction dialog box, where you'll see a preview of your image with a grid overlay. If needed, use the buttons on the top-left edge of the dialog box to remove distortion, straighten the image to a new horizontal or vertical axis, or reposition the grid. Otherwise, in the Auto Correction tab, select the camera used to create the image from the Camera Make menu, and then choose the appropriate model and lens from the Camera Model and Lens Model menus. After making your lens selection, click the checkboxes as needed to include corrections for geometric distortion, chromatic aberration, and vignette.

> HINT: If you don't see the lens make or model that you need, click around until you can find something comparable.

STEP 3   In the Custom tab, add or subtract additional lens correction settings. For instance, you can use the Vignette slider to add or subtract a vignette to your image. You may also want to adjust the Vertical and Horizontal Perspective sliders to correct distortions, like the pole in the example. Click OK to apply your settings to your image. Figure 26-2 shows the corrected image with an added vignette.

Figure 26-2

TECHNIQUE

27

EXTENDING DEPTH OF FIELD

WITH DIGITAL PHOTOGRAPHY, there are no excuses for not taking enough photographs. Even so, you might still take a series of shots where no single image has the exact depth of field you're aiming for. In fact, you may wish that you could easily combine several elements from a handful of different shots into one final composite image.

You certainly could do that, painstakingly creating layer masks and blending each part into a final whole. But why go to that much trouble when you can use the combined power of the Auto-Align and Auto-Blend features to seamlessly blend the best parts of several images into one composite shot?

STEP 1 For this exercise, you will need at least three images with varying depths of field, like the spoon photos shown in Figure 27-1.

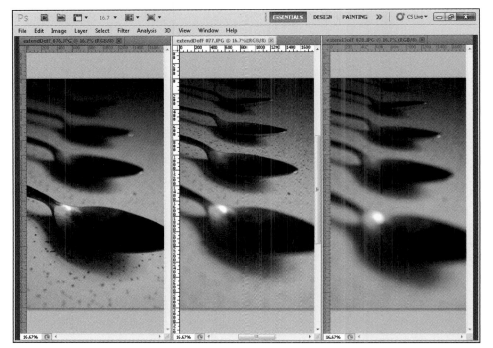

Figure 27-1

There are several ways to add multiple images into a single document, but for this technique, you're going to choose **File > Scripts > Load Images into Stack**. When the Load Layers dialog box opens set to Use Files, click the Browse button to navigate to and select the images in your series. Leave the two options at the bottom of the dialog box unchecked and click OK to load all the images onto separate layers within a new document.

STEP 2 Press Alt+Ctrl+A/Option+⌘+A to select all the layers in the Layers panel. Then select **Edit > Auto-Align Layers**. This nifty little feature automatically places all of your layers in the best position for the next step.

STEP 3 Select **Edit > Auto-Blend Layers**, choose the Stack Images option, make sure the Seamless Tones and Colors checkbox is selected, and click OK. Photoshop will then blend the selected layers based on their content to produce a single composited image made from the best parts of each layer. Figure 27-2 shows the finished product. Take a look at the Layers panel to see the complexity of the masks. It's really quite remarkable that all this happens automatically!

> HINT: Keep in mind that the quality of the outcome depends on the quality of the starting images, so some image sets will work better than others.

Figure 27-2

28

TECHNIQUE

EDITING WITH THE VANISHING POINT

EDITING IMAGES WITH perspective planes—like the side of a building, flooring, or some other rectangular object—can be, well, a real pain. For instance, you may need to add a window to the side of a building, eliminate an element from a scene, or remove a door. However, if your edits aren't correctly scaled and placed, the final image can look fake and obviously doctored.

Vanishing Point makes editing perspectives trouble-free by allowing you to create planes for your image and apply edits to those planes, such as copying and pasting, transforming, painting, and cloning. As if by magic, all your edits area applied within this same perspective! This is the perfect technique for photo retouching.

STEP 1   To learn how to edit with Vanishing Point, open an image in your workspace with a strong perspective plane, like the building pictured in Figure 28-1. For this technique, you will add and remove windows on the side of the building, but keep in mind that you can follow the same general principles to reposition objects and even paste copied selections into the picture plane from other scenes.

Figure 28-1

STEP 2   Select **Filter > Vanishing Point** to open the Vanishing Point dialog box. The first thing you'll want to do is set up a perspective plane by selecting the Create Plane tool (C) from row of buttons along the top-left edge. To do that, determine where you want the plane to fall across your image and then click on each of the four corners of the imagined plane in succession. With the fourth click, you will see a perspective grid appear across your image (see Figure 28-2).

To adjust how the plane sits atop your image, click any of the grid's corner or midpoint nodes. To step backwards (undo) or delete a plane, press the Backspace/Delete key.

> HINT: If you will be editing more than one plane within your image, add more planes as needed with the Create Plane tool. To "tear off" planes from existing ones, select the Create Plane tool and Ctrl+drag/⌘+drag an edge node.

STEP 3   To clone an area of your image within the plane, press S to select the Stamp tool, and then Alt+click to set the clone source (sample area) within the image you'd like to copy. To paint a copy of the sourced image into another area of your scene, slowly click and drag in a back-and-forth, wiping motion until the image looks the way you want it to. For example, Figure 28-2 shows the addition of a third window on the top-right side of the house along one of the three planes created for this image.

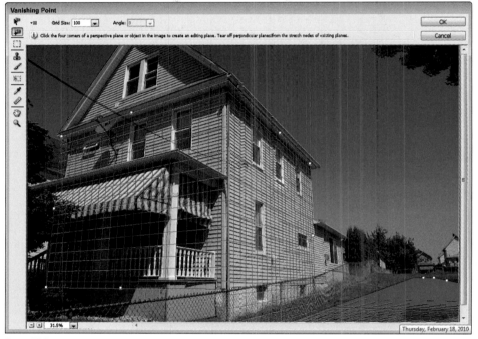

Figure 28-2

STEP 4   To fill a selection with another part of your image, select the Marquee tool (M), set the Move Mode menu to Destination, make a selection within a plane, and Ctrl+drag/⌘+drag the pointer from within the selection onto the area you want to fill.

Other editing features include:

- pasting an object from the Clipboard
- creating and editing a selection
- painting with sampled pixels or sampled color
- transforming a selection

When you are finished making changes, click OK to close the dialog box and continue working in Photoshop.

> HINT: *After you work in Vanishing Point, you can keep working on the image and even re-enter Vanishing Point to make further edits along the same perspective plane. To save the perspective plane in your image, be sure to save your document in PSD, TIFF, or JPEG format.*

29

MAKING PANORAMAS WITH PHOTOMERGE

TAKING IN A scene with one's own eyes has always been superior to seeing a place in a photograph. Not only that, but photos often capture only part of the scene without really conveying a sense of what it felt like to actually be there. Panoramas, however, do tend to impart some of that mysterious "being there" quality.

With Photoshop's Photomerge command, you can now create stunning panoramas within seconds. All you need is a set of digital images with a unified focal length, viewpoint, and exposure, as well as edges that overlap between 40% and 70%.

STEP 1   This exercise requires three to six images with overlapping edges, like the set of pictures shown in Figure 29-1.

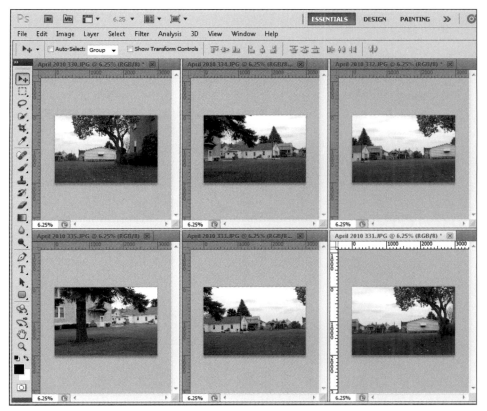

Figure 29-1

Since the entire process is automated, there's very little for you to do! To start, select **File > Automate > Photomerge**, and when the dialog box opens, select the Auto Layout option, which will apply the best layout option to your images to produce the best results. In the Source Files area, choose Files or Folder from the Use menu and click the Browse button to navigate to and select the images in your series.

> HINT: *To select a series of images that are already open in Photoshop, click the Add Open Files button instead.*

If your original images have vignettes or lens distortion, check the Vignette Removal and/or Geometric Distortion Correction boxes. Finally, click OK to merge your images.

STEP 2   While you are waiting, Photoshop sequentially opens each of the images, searches for common areas based on content, and blends each layer with the next in a single file to build your ultimate panorama. Look at Figure 29-2 to see the final results, along with how each image layer is masked in the Layers panel to create a unified photograph.

Figure 29-2

FAKING HIGH DYNAMIC RANGE WITH HDR TONING

HIGH DYNAMIC RANGE (HDR) is a type of picture that is insanely detailed and colored, typically created by shooting several photographs of the same subject and digitally merging them. For example, you could take one normally exposed, one overexposed, and one underexposed image and combine them in Photoshop to make an ultra-crisp, detailed, and intense HDR image.

Although taking and merging all those photos is a feat often best left to a professional photographer, that doesn't mean you have to give up on the idea of using Photoshop to fake it. In the past, the normal workflow for faking HDR involved changing your image to LAB color, converting it into a Smart Object (to make editing non-destructive), pumping up the shadows/highlights, adjusting the curves, and adding sharpening with the High Pass filter. Now, with the HDR Toning command, you can fudge your way there in one simple step.

STEP 1   Open a photograph in Photoshop that you'd like to give the HDR look to. The image can be of anything you like, such as a landscape, a portrait, or a still life.

STEP 2   Select **Image** > **Adjustments** > **HDR Toning** to open the HDR Toning dialog box. Choose Custom from the Preset menu and Local Adaptation from the Method menu. Here you can edit the Edge Glow, Tone and Detail Color, and Toning Curve, and Histogram. There are no "right" answers for how to tone your image, so play around and adjust some of the sliders until the image looks HDR to you. Typically, you'll get the best results when you adjust the Gamma, Exposure, and Detail sliders before you lighten or darken shadows and highlights and add vibrance and saturation. When you're finished, click OK.

Figure 30-1 shows an example of a normal photo before (left) and after (right) applying HDR Toning.

Figure 30-1

Of course, you don't have to stop there. You can push your image beyond normal into the realm of the surreal with HDR Toning and Adjustment layers. Figure 30-2 shows a comparison of an original image next to a version with HDR, Levels, and Hue/Saturation Adjustments, and another with HDR and Levels Adjustment.

Figure 30-2

TECHNIQUE

31

CREATING 3D OBJECTS FROM 2D ART

ONE OF THE big features in Photoshop that Adobe has been improving upon over the past few releases is giving you the ability to create, edit, and export 3D images. As of CS4 Extended, you can now quickly transform your flat 2D artwork into a variety of shapes including a cone, cube, cube wrap, cylinder, donut, hat, pyramid, ring, soda can, sphere, spherical panorama, and wine bottle! Granted, some of these shapes are a little more refined than others, but the cool news is that you can effectively wrap your artwork around them in just a few simple steps.

STEP 1   To see how this feature works, open any file in your Photoshop workspace. It can be a photograph, a logo, an advertisement, or flattened label art like the image shown in Figure 31-1.

Figure 31-1

STEP 2   Select **3D > New Shape From Layer > Soda Can** and watch as Photoshop creates a three-dimensional soda can and wraps your artwork around it! You can now add lights, cameras, paint, and any other transformation and editing you would normally add to a 3D image.

STEP 3   Notice the 3D Axis icon at the top-left edge of your document window, as seen in Figure 31-2. Press K to select the Object Rotate tool, click the X-, Y-, or Z-axis points on the Axis icon to choose the orientation you'd like to modify, and then click and drag on your 3D image to rotate, roll, drag, slide, and scale different aspects of your 3D image.

Figure 31-2

STEP 4   To modify the camera angle, Press N to select the Camera Rotate tool, click the X-, Y-, or Z-axis points on the Axis icon to choose the camera orientation, and then click and drag on your 3D image to orbit, roll, pan, walk, and zoom different aspects of your 3D image.

STEP 5   To apply lighting to your 3D object, select Window > 3D to open the 3D panel, click the Create A New Light button at the bottom of the 3D panel (it's the New icon next to the Trash icon), and select the type of light you'd like to apply (point, spot, infinite, or image based) from the pop-up menu. You can then adjust the settings for the new light source in the 3D panel.

STEP 6   When you have finished editing the 3D object, continue working in Photoshop until you have completed your layout. Figure 31-3 shows this 3D image in an advertisement.

Figure 31-3

TECHNIQUE

32

CORRECTING EXPOSURE WITH TONE-PROTECTED DODGE AND BURN

POSSIBLY TWO OF the most under-utilized tools in Photoshop's toolbar are the Dodge and Burn tools. Created to simulate traditional darkroom exposure techniques, the more you paint over an area in your image with these tools, the more you can selectively lighten or darken parts of your image. In addition to lightening underexposed areas of a photo and darkening overexposed areas, these tools can also help you improve overall exposure, direct the viewer's eye to key areas (by subduing irrelevant elements), and add dramatic impact to a scene through light and shadow.

Now, it could be that these tools haven't been very popular because they can only be applied directly (and therefore destructively) to a layer. However, did you know that you actually can apply these techniques non-destructively? Not only that, but (since CS4) you can also protect skin tones to avoid skin turning orange or gray. Read on to learn how you can create tone-protected images with the new and improved Dodge and Burn tools.

STEP 1   Open an image in the Photoshop workspace that contains areas of over and underexposure, or areas of intense shadow and highlight, like the child photo shown in Figure 32-1. It's a nice enough picture, but the child's features are obscured by dark shadows and bright highlights, and the window scene is a bit distracting.

Figure 32-1

STEP 2   Press Shift+Ctrl+N/Shift+⌘+N to create a new non-destructive layer. When the New Layer dialog box opens, Name the layer **D&B**, set the Mode to Soft Light, and check the Fill with Soft-Light-neutral color box. You are going to apply your Dodge and Burn strokes to this layer.

STEP 3   Press O to select the Dodge tool and use the settings on the Options bar to determine the tool's brush size and hardness. Select Shadows from the Range menu and set the Exposure to 25%. Leave the Protect Tones feature selected, as this will help eliminate those strange orange and gray skin tone casts the old Dodge and Burn tools would often create.

> HINT: To quickly adjust the brush size and hardness as you work, press the left ([) and right (]) bracket keys to increase or decrease the brush diameter and press Shift+[or Shift+] to soften or harden the brush edges.

Drag your tool across the shadow areas in several passes until the shadow areas are lightened enough to see the details you'd like to reveal.

STEP 4   Press Shift+O to toggle to the Burn tool, then on the Options bar choose High-lights from the Range menu, and set the Exposure to 25%. Drag your brush a few times across the highlight areas to reduce the glare.

Toggle back and forth between the Dodge and Burn tools, adjusting the Shadows, Midtones, and Highlights ranges until you have the image the way you like it. If there are any distracting areas within your image that pull the eye away from the main focal area, darken them using the Burn tool set to the Shadow Range. For instance, in the picture in Figure 32-1 the left part of the background can be darkened a little more to make the child's smile more of the focal point.

> HINT: Since highlights tend to catch the eye more readily than shadows, try increasing the exposure when working in the shadows range and decreasing the exposure when working with highlights.

STEP 5   To help make the bright background area less distracting, duplicate the image layer (Ctrl+J/⌘+J), select **Filter > Blur > Gaussian Blur**, set the Radius to about 16 px (if your starting image is 300 dpi, otherwise, select a smaller radius), and then click OK. Press E to select the Eraser tool and with a large, soft-edged brush, erase everything but the bright background area you want to keep, as shown in Figure 32-2.

Figure 32-2

STEP 6   The last step is sharpening. Select the main image layer and select **Filter > Sharpen > Unsharp Mask**. Set the Amount to about 150%, the Radius to 2.3 px, the Threshold to 10 levels, and then click OK. Figure 32-3 shows the original image before (top) and after (bottom) correcting the exposure, blurring the background, and sharpening. Keep in mind that your particular image may require more or less sharpening than the example, so use your best judgment to choose what looks right to you.

Figure 32-3

TECHNIQUE 33

ADJUSTING SHADOWS AND HIGHLIGHTS

IN ADDITION TO using Curves and Levels to correct the tonality of your photographs, you can also play with the Shadows/Highlights feature to help recover details in the shadow and highlight areas of a backlit image. This feature works a little bit like the Recovery and Fill Light sliders in Adobe Camera Raw, plus it also has additional controls to help with improving the blown out areas caused by a camera flash and lightening shadows in well exposed photographs. Best of all, you can apply Shadows/Highlights as a non-destructive filter if you first convert your image into a Smart Object.

STEP 1   Start this project by opening a backlit image in Photoshop. If you don't have one to work with but you do have a digital camera, take a picture of someone or something indoors in front of a bright window. For example, the picture in Figure 33-1 was shot facing the window inside of a passenger car of an old steam engine train.

Figure 33-1

STEP 2   Select your image layer and choose **Filter > Convert for Smart Filters**. Converting the layer into a Smart Object lets you apply the Shadows/Highlight adjustment as a nondestructive Smart Filter that acts a lot like an adjustment layer, including having its own layer mask that you can use to selectively edit certain parts of the layer. For instance, you may want to reveal shadow areas of the subject but leave the background darkened.

STEP 3   To add the Smart Filter to your Smart Object, select **Image > Adjustments > Shadows/Highlight.** At once, the Shadows/Highlight dialog box opens and the Smart Filter is added to your layer, as shown in Figure 33-2. If you happen to see a smaller version of the dialog box, click the Show More Options checkbox to reveal the rest of the sliders.

Shadows/Highlights

Shadows

Amount: 26 %

Tonal Width: 67 %

Radius: 49 px

OK
Cancel
Load...
Save...
☑ Preview

Highlights

Amount: 41 %

Tonal Width: 73 %

Radius: 90 px

Adjustments

Color Correction: +31

Midtone Contrast: -5

Black Clip: 0.01 %

White Clip: 0.01 %

Save As Defaults
☑ Show More Options

LAYERS

Normal   Opacity: 100%

Lock: ☐ ✎ ✛ 🔒   Fill: 100%

👁 After

👁 Smart Filters

👁 Shadows/Highlights

👁 Before

133

Figure 33-2

STEP 4   If you like, use the settings shown in the Shadows/Highlights dialog box in Figure 33-2 as a starting point for your image. Otherwise, experiment until the image looks right to you:

- In the Shadows area, shift the Amount slider to the left to darken or to the right to brighten the areas with shadows. The Tonal Width sets the range of values affected by the Amount slider. The lower or higher the number, the smaller or greater are the shadows areas that are affected. Keep the width somewhat narrow to produce the best results. The Radius softens the edges of the Amount and Tonal Width.
- In the Highlights area, shift the Amount slider to darken the brightest areas, the Tonal Width to set the range of the values affected by the Amount, and the Radius to soften the edges.
- In the Adjustments area, apply a bit of Color Correction and Midtone Contrast to improve the overall image quality.
- When finished, click OK to close the dialog box.

    HINT: To return to the Shadows/Highlights dialog box at any time to make further adjustments, double-click the Shadows/Highlights filter effect name in the Layers panel.

STEP 5   To adjust the strength of the Shadows/Highlight Smart Filter affecting your image, select the Smart Filter mask thumbnail in your Layers panel and use the Paint Brush tool (B) to paint across your image with a black or white brush to either conceal or reveal areas of the filter. You may also want to apply a Sharpening filter to your main image to sharpen some of the details. Figure 33-3 shows the example image before and after using the Shadows/Highlight Smart Filter.

Figure 33-3

TECHNIQUE

34

MASTERING THE PUPPET WARP

NEW TO CS5 is the freaky and amazing Puppet Warp filter, which overlays your layer with an intricate visual mesh that you can tweak and distort to transform the shape and position of the various elements within your layer. The transformations you make with this new feature can range from crazy to restrained depending on your needs. Use it for subtle image retouching like arching an eyebrow or pouting a lip, as well as shifting angles, bending objects, and distorting. This tool works on photographs, vector shapes, text, and both layer and vector masks! You can even apply Puppet Warp distortions non-destructively by first converting your layer into a Smart Object.

STEP 1 Open an image in your workspace that you would like to transform. To learn the Puppet Warp tool, choose an image that only needs a slight transformation, such as a simple close-up of nature like the example in Figure 34-1. Once you become proficient with the tool's features, you can tackle projects that are more ambitious.

Figure 34-1

STEP 2 Puppet Warp can't be applied to a locked background layer but it can be applied either destructively to a regular layer or mask, or non-destructively to a Smart Object layer. Select your image layer or mask and choose **Filter > Convert for Smart Filters**. Then select **Edit > Puppet Warp**.

> *HINT: If you plan to edit just a small region within your image, zoom in to that area before selecting Edit > Puppet Warp.*

STEP 3 In the Options bar you can set the elasticity and spacing of mesh points with the Mode and Density menus. Set the mode to Rigid and the density to Normal. To help keep the image in place as you warp, set the Expansion menu to 20 px.

The Puppet Warp mesh works by a system of pins, which serve as anchors for the transformations. Click to add pins in each of the four corners of your image, and then add several more pins around the area in your image you want to adjust. Figure 34-2 shows the example image with the mesh and pins.

> *HINT: If you find the mesh distracting, deselect the Show Mesh option on the Options bar. You can also temporarily hide the pins by pressing the H key.*

Figure 34-2

STEP 4   To warp the mesh, click and drag the pins to their new position. To move several pins at once, Shift+click on the pins you would like to select before repositioning. Press Alt+drag/Option+drag to rotate the mesh around a selected pin. You can even use the arrow keys to reposition selected pins.

Use the icons on the right edge of the Options bar to remove all pins and start over, cancel puppet warp (Esc) to undo any changes you have made while using the tool, or commit puppet warp (Enter/Return) to keep and apply your transformations.

STEP 5   To clean up the edges and otherwise control which parts of the filter are affecting your Smart Object layer, select the Smart Filter mask thumbnail in your Layers panel and use the Paint Brush tool (B) to paint across your image with a black or white brush to either conceal or reveal areas of the filter. As a last step, apply a sharpening filter. Figure 34-3 shows the sample image before and after using Puppet Warp.

Figure 34-3

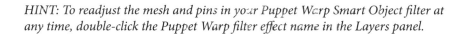

HINT: To readjust the mesh and pins in your Puppet Warp Smart Object filter at any time, double-click the Puppet Warp filter effect name in the Layers panel.

USING THE MIXER BRUSH AND BRISTLE TIPS

TECHNIQUE 35

FROM TIME TO time, Adobe introduces new tools to the Photoshop toolbox. In CS5 you have two new Paint Brush options—the Mixer Brush and Bristle Tips—that can really enhance the way you paint. Bristle Tips actually look like real paintbrush tips to help you create more realistic brush strokes. Likewise, the Mixer Brush helps you make more natural-looking paint strokes by mixing colors on the canvas, blending two or more colors on the brush, and painting with both wet and dry brush strokes.

STEP 1   Start by opening an image in your workspace that has some areas you would like to paint on, like the winterberries image shown in Figure 35-1. The berries look a bit weathered from the cold, so you will plump them back up using the Mixer Brush with Bristle Tips.

Figure 35-1

STEP 2   Duplicate the background layer by pressing Ctrl+J/⌘+J, and with your copied layer selected, select **Window > Brush** to open the Brush panel. This is where you preview and select the new Bristle Tips available for your brushes. Select the 25 px Round Point brush and notice the new Bristle Brush Preview window at the left of your screen. Use the preview and the various brush settings to create a brush that has the precise bristle characteristics you need. For instance, you may want to adjust the bristle density by setting bristles to 45%, and set the brush thickness to 23%.

STEP 3   Click and hold on the regular Brush tool until you see the pop-up menu, and then select the Mixer Brush from the bottom of the list. Unfortunately you can't use the Mixer Brush on a Smart Object for non-destructive editing, so before you proceed create a new layer (Shift+Ctrl+N/Shift+⌘+N) to work on and select Sample All Layers from the brush Options bar.

For your paint color, you can either click the Color swatch on the Options bar to mix a custom color or sample a color from your image, or load "paint" into the brush reservoir by Alt+clicking/Option+clicking on the canvas, much like you would sample the source with the Clone Stamp. In this example, sample the berries to load a berry red color into the brush.

STEP 4   To paint, simply drag your brush across the canvas in a series of strokes, as you would with a normal paintbrush. You can control the amount of paint in your brush using the Wet, Load, Mix, and Flow menus on the Options bar, or by choosing one of the presets, such as Moist, Light Mix, from the Blending Brush Combo pop-up menu.

To help you paint in a more natural way, toggle on and off the Load the Brush After Each Stroke and Clean the Brush After Each Stoke buttons on the Options bar, as needed.

How far you go in a painterly direction is entirely up to you. You can keep your painting to a minimum or go all the way, turning your photo into a painted image. Figure 35-2 shows a version with only plumper berries (top) and another with the full painted effect (bottom).

Figure 35-2

TECHNIQUE 36

USING ADOBE 3D REPOUSSÉ

PHOTOSHOP CS5'S NEW Repoussé feature puts the power of 3D in your hands. Not only can you swiftly turn your 2D text and art into 3D mesh objects that you can reposition in space, but you can also extrude the shapes and inflate their surfaces to create more realistic image depth and contours. Although the repoussé technique is not available for rasterized text or shape layers, it will work on text layers, shape layers, layer masks, selected paths, and selections.

STEP 1   Select **File > New** to open the New document dialog box. From Preset choose Photo; from Size choose Portrait 5×7, and click OK.

STEP 2   Select the Horizontal Type tool (T) and enter the word **MASK** in Bimini Bold 150 pt black (or another font of your choice) across the top of the file. Next, select the Custom Shape tool (U), select a shape (such as a fleur de lys) from the Shape menu on the Options bar, drag out a shape, and center the shape above the letter A, as illustrated in Figure 36-1.

Figure 36-1

STEP 3   Ctrl+click/⌘+click the thumbnail of text layer to select the text, and then Shift+Ctrl+click/Shift+⌘+click the thumbnail mask of the shape layer to add that shape to the selection.

To convert these selected layers into a 3D repoussé object, select **3D > Repoussé > Current Selection**. When the Repoussé dialog box opens, don't be alarmed by all the options; although there are a lot of settings, you'll only be configuring a few of them for this technique.

> HINT: Repoussé is a feature-rich addition to CS5. To get the most out of using this tool, be sure to spend some time playing around with the different settings in this dialog box. The more time you spend experimenting, the more you will discover how to manipulate your layers effectively.

Starting on the top-left under Repoussé Shape Presents, scroll down the list and select Inflate. Next, you'll apply patterns to the face and sides of your image. From Materials, click the Front menu and select Satin Black, and from the Sides menu, select Tiles Checkerboard. Then, to change the lighting under Scene Settings, select Shape 3 from the View menu. Your image should now look like the example in Figure 36-2.

Figure 36-2

STEP 4   If you would like to adjust the size and position of your repoussé object, select the 3D Object Rotate tool (K) from the Tool bar to click and drag the object into a new orientation. You may also use the other 3D tools on the Options bar to rotate, roll, drag, slide, and scale along the X, Y, and Z axes.

To edit any of the other settings in a repoussé layer, select the layer and choose Edit in Repoussé from the layer's context menu.

Figure 36-3 shows an example of how you might use the example repoussé object in a print layout.

Figure 36-3

TECHNIQUE 37

MERGING EXPOSURES WITH AUTO-BLEND

COMBINE THE BEST of several images with different exposures into a single image using the Auto-Blend command. Your images can be slightly overlapping or simply shot at several different exposures to make the best of less than perfect lighting conditions. This exercise shows you how easy it is to merge several files into one.

STEP 1   To perform this technique you will need a series of two or more photographic images of the same subject with different exposures, like the canned goods and condiments shown in Figure 37-1.

Figure 37-1

STEP 2   Begin by selecting **Scripts > Load Images Into Stack**. When the Load Layers dialog box opens, click the Browse button to navigate to and select your image files, click the Attempt to Automatically Align Source Images checkbox, and then click OK to load all the images onto separate layers within a new document, as illustrated in Figure 37-2.

> HINT: *To select a series of images that are already open in the Photoshop workspace, click the Add Open Files button instead.*

148

Figure 37-2

STEP 3   Next you'll perform the exposure merge. First press Alt+Ctrl+A/Option+⌘+A to select all the layers in the Layers panel. Then select **Edit > Auto-Blend Layers**, choose the Stack Images option, make sure the Seamless Tones and Colors checkbox is selected, and click OK. Photoshop will then blend the selected layers based on their content to produce a single composited image made from the best parts of each layer. Figure 37-3 shows the final blended exposure.

Figure 37-3

149

USING CONTENT-AWARE FILL AND SPOT HEALING

PHOTOSHOP CS5'S NEW Content-Aware Fill introduces you to a new way of removing blemishes and imperfections from your photographs. With this feature, you can effortlessly fill any selection with similar image content sampled from around the selected area. Combine this feature with the improved Spot Healing Brush for fast and seamlessly integrated photo retouching.

STEP 1   Open the portrait file you want to apply this effect to and zoom into the area that needs retouching. For example, you may want to eliminate a mole, freckle, wrinkle, discoloration, or other skin blemish, as with the large beauty mark on the man's right cheek in Figure 38-1.

Figure 38-1

STEP 2   To use the Content-Aware feature, press L to choose the Lasso tool to make a tight selection around the area to be edited, then select **Edit > Fill** (Shift+F5). When the Fill dialog box opens, choose Content-Aware from the Use menu and click OK. Photoshop then samples other pixels surrounding the selection to fill the selection with replacement pixels, as illustrated in Figure 38-2. Keep in mind that this technique works best when the selection area is rather small; larger selections can sometimes result in unnatural fills.

STEP 3   Press J to select the Spot Healing Brush tool, choose a 50-px soft-edged (0% hardness) brush, and select Content-Aware as the type on the Options bar. Then paint in simple clicks or small, delicate strokes across the areas that need retouching.

While you're at it, you may want to play around with the two other Healing Brush Type options on the Options bar. Use Proximity Match to make Photoshop use pixels around the selection edges for the patch, or select Create Texture to have Photoshop use the pixels within the selection to create a texture for the patch.

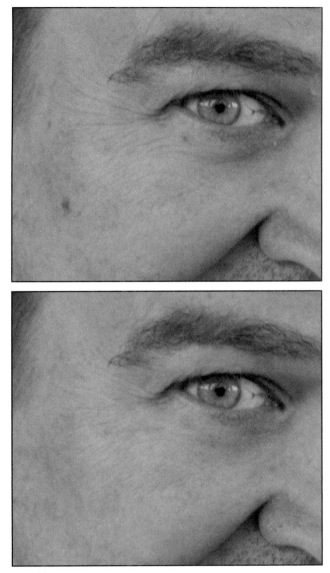

Figure 38-2

HINT: For retouching problem areas like moles, you'll achieve better results using the Clone Stamp and Smudge tools.

STEP 4   Continue working around the image, alternating between the Spot Healing Brush tool and Content-Aware Fill technique until you have finished retouching the image. As a final step, apply a little sharpening to your image using the Smart Sharpen or Unsharp Mask filter. To give you an idea at how dramatic your changes can be, look at the before and after pictures in Figure 38-3.

Figure 38-3

153

III TEXT EFFECTS

TECHNIQUE

39

ADDING TYPE IN A SHAPE

ALTHOUGH TECHNICALLY PHOTOSHOP is not a page layout program, many people use the program to design Web layouts, Web banner ads, postcards, business cards, logos, and the occasional print advertisement. In addition to adding point type (click and type) and paragraph type (click and drag to create a bounding box, and then type) with the Horizontal Type tool, you can also add type inside a shape. In other words, you can add text to shapes created with any of the Shape tools (U) such as the Ellipse or Custom Shape tool, path shapes created from the selected outlines of an object on a layer, mask, or channel, or shapes created from a saved path.

STEP 1   The example shown in this technique requires the use of a free geographical font called GeoBats designed by the generous Daniel Zadorozny of Iconian.com. Visit http://iconian.com/g.html to download and install a copy of the font on your computer. If Photoshop is open, close and reopen it to gain access to the newly installed font.

STEP 2   Select **File > New** to open the New document dialog box. Under Preset choose Photo, set the Width to 5.25 inches, the Height to 5 inches, and click OK. Next, press T to select the Horizontal Type tool and on the Options bar, set the font to GeoBats, the Size to 68 pt, and the Color to something bright and easy to see, like a red or green. Click your cursor once in the center of your file and press the lowercase s key to insert the continent of Australia.

STEP 3   Ctrl+click/⌘+click the type layer's thumbnail to select the shape, click over to the Paths panel, and click the Make Work Path from Selection button at the bottom of the panel. Double-click the new Work Path layer and name the path *Australia*.

Now return to the Layers panel, hide the visibility of the Australia type layer, press T to select the Type tool, and set the font to Georgia, Regular, 8 pt, Sharp, with the color set to a rusty brown with the Hex value of #92500e. Click inside the Australia path outline (the dotted lines around the cursor should be round, not square or linear before you click) to set the insertion point, and type or paste in enough copied text to fill the shape, as shown in Figure 39-1.

Figure 39-1

HINT: With this particular shape outline, which has two unconnected pieces, your text will not automatically flow into the island of Tazmania. Therefore, to add text there you will need to reselect the work path and enter a second text layer directly to that shape.

STEP 4   Return to the Paths panel and Ctrl+click/⌘+click the Australia path layer's thumbnail to select the shape again. Shift back to the Layers panel, press Shift+Ctrl+I/ Shift+⌘+I to inverse the selection, and choose **Layer > New Fill Layer > Solid Color**. In the color dialog box that opens, enter a value of #0797b1 in the Hex field, and click OK. Your layout now has a blue background with text flowing inside the shape of Australia with a white background.

STEP 5   To further define the continent shape you'll add a drop shadow effect. Ctrl+click/ ⌘+click the thumbnail on the Color Fill layer to select the shape again, press Shift+Ctrl+I/ Shift+⌘+I to inverse the selection, and then choose **Layer > New Fill Layer > Solid Color**. This time fill the mask with white (#ffffff) and click OK. Adjust the Fill of this layer to 0%, and then select **Layer > Layer Style > Drop Shadow**, set the Angle to 120°, the Distance to 10 px, the Size to 16 px, and click OK. Figure 39-2 shows how your image should look thus far.

Figure 39-2

STEP 6   For the final touches, as seen in Figure 39-3, add a sunny gradient to the inside of the continent, add a talk bubble shape, put some catchy text inside of it, and add a text layer with URL to learn more about Australia.

Figure 39-3

40

USING TYPE ON A PATH

WITH PHOTOSHOP, YOU can add type on nearly any kind of path including shape paths created with any of the Shape tools (U), work paths and clipping paths created from selections in the Paths panel, and open and closed paths created with the Pen and Freeform Pen tools.

STEP 1 Select **File > New** to open the New document dialog box. Under Preset, choose Photo, set the width to 4 inches, the height to 3 inches, and click OK. You're going to create some label artwork for a pickle jar.

STEP 2 Select the Rectangle tool (U) and draw out a large rectangle shape in the center of your canvas that is roughly 3 inches wide by 2.15 inches tall. Double-click the rectangle layer's Color Fill thumbnail on the Layers panel and change the color to #ddd9cc.

STEP 3 Select the Custom Shape tool (U) from the toolbar, click the Custom Shape menu to view the pop-up panel, click the arrow in the upper-right corner of the panel, and select the Banners and Awards category to load those shapes into your menu. When the dialog box opens asking if you want to replace or append your current shapes, choose Append. Scroll down the menu a little and select the flag shape. Drag out a flag shape that spans across the rectangle from edge to edge and fill this shape with #3c622d, as illustrated in Figure 40-1.

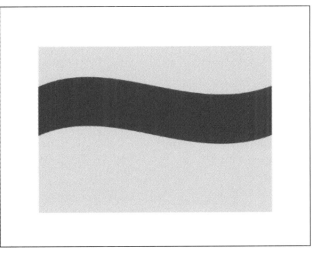

Figure 40-1

STEP 4 Press T to select the Type tool, and set the font to Lucida Handwriting Italic, the size to 36 pt, and the color to white. Hover your cursor above the top edge of the shape and when the dotted lines around the cursor turn into a straight line (as if the cursor is surfing along the path), click once and begin typing the word **HARVEY'S** in all caps.

Use the Path Selection tool (A) to adjust the flow of your text along the path so that it flows from left to right along the top edge of the shape. Then use the Move tool (V) to position the text inside the green flag shape, as shown in Figure 40-2.

Figure 40-2

STEP 5 Next, you to create a simple curved path for some text above the top green flag shape that mimics that curve. Press P to select the Pen tool, and above the left edge of the H in Harvey's, click and drag upward and to the right about one inch, release your mouse, and click and drag again above the right edge of the R, dragging slightly downward to the right.

Press T to select the Type tool, and set the font to a script such as Rage Italic, the size to 14pt, and the color to #867143. Hover your cursor above the top edge of the curve and when the dotted lines around the cursor turn into a straight line (as if the cursor is surfing along the path), click once and type **Premium Quality**, as illustrated in Figure 40-3.

Figure 40-3

STEP 6   For the final set of embellishments, add a little more text and some layer styles. In the fonts of your choice, add the words **Since 1972**, **KOSHER ORGANIC**, and **DILL PICKLES** to the layout.

Select the flag layer, choose **Layer > Layer Style > Drop Shadow**, set the angle to 105°, the distance to 8 px and the size to 8 px. Add a Bevel and Emboss Style with the style set to Outer Bevel and the size set to 14 px. Add a satin style with the blending mode set to Soft Light, the angle at 19°, the distance at 27 px, the size at 9 px, and the contour set to Ring. Last, apply a Stroke style with the size set to 9 px, the position set to Inside, and the color set to #ddb516. Then click OK to finish.

Your label art is complete! Now pop it onto a pickle jar, throw in a background gradient, add a reflection and a zippy tagline, and you're finished. Figure 40-4 shows the completed artwork used in a pickle ad.

Figure 40-4

TECHNIQUE 41

CREATING SHINY PLASTIC TEXT

FROM AN ADVERTISING standpoint, there is nothing quite as shiny and seductive as big, glossy, plastic lettering. Although some may say that it has been overdone as of late, when used professionally and tastefully (such as within the advertising industry) it can be really attractive.

Maybe it's the reflective surface, the puffy bevel, or the smooth edges. Whatever it is that makes it so appealing, it's fun and easy to give your text the plastic look in Photoshop.

STEP 1 Select **File** > **New** to open the New document dialog box. Under Preset, choose Photo, set the width to 7 inches and height to 2 inches, and click OK. You're going to create the plastic text effect in the menu design shown in Figure 41-1.

Figure 41-1

HINT: To learn how to create the entire reflective surface menu design in Figure 41-1, see Technique #51, "Making Magical Reflected Surfaces."

STEP 2 Press T to select the Type tool, set the font to a thick display font such as Gill Sans Ultra Bold in 80 pt with the color set to a Hex value of #ff0000, and type the word **BURGER** in all caps across your document.

Click the Add Layer Style button at the bottom of the Layers panel and choose Bevel and Emboss from the pop-up menu. When the dialog box opens, set the style to Inner Bevel, the technique to Smooth, the depth to 150%, the size to 18 px, the angle to 120°, the altitude to 40°, the Highlight Mode's opacity to 100%, and the Shadow Mode's opacity to 0%. For the Gloss Contour, click the down arrow to open the Contour picker and click the arrow in the upper-right corner to select the Contours option. When the dialog box opens asking if you want to replace or append your contours, click Append. Then scroll down the list, select Ring – Triple, and put a check in the Anti-Aliased checkbox.

Now select the Contour category below the Bevel and Emboss style, choose Shallow Slope – Valley from the Contour picker, and click the Anti-Aliased checkbox.

Don't close the Layer Style dialog box yet.

STEP 3 To put a shine around the outer edges of the letters, add an Inner Glow style. Change the blending mode to Multiply, change the color to #4f2409, set the source to Edge, and change the size to 23 px. Now click OK to close the Layer Style dialog box. At this point, your text should look something like the example in Figure 41-2.

Figure 41-2

STEP 4 Press Ctrl+J/⌘+J to duplicate the text layer, and then reselect the original text layer to make a few more tweaks. Double-click the Layer Style *fx* icon on the right side of the original layer to reopen the Layer Style dialog box and add a stroke with the size set to 9 px, the position set to Outside, and the fill color set to #5d1616.

To add more depth to the lettering on the original layer, reselect the Bevel and Emboss style, change the bevel style from Inner Bevel to Stroke Emboss, and change the depth to 32%.

For the final touch, change the Bevel and Emboss Gloss Contour from Ring – Triple to one of the other contours, such as Terraced, Valley – High, or the one used in this example, Shallow Slope – Valley. Then adjust the Highlight Mode's opacity to 100% and the Shadow Mode's opacity to 55%. Et voilà, c'est ça! Figure 41-3 shows a detail of the final lettering.

Figure 41-3

TECHNIQUE

42

ARCHING TEXT AROUND A CENTER POINT

ADDING TEXT TO a path in Photoshop is remarkably fast and simple to learn, as you discovered in Technique #40, "Using Type on a Path." But what if you need to create a layout with text flowing around a center point, with two lines of type that both flow from left to right (see Figure 42-1)? That can be a little tricky—especially if you want the outer edges of the letters to align. Fortunately, there's a straightforward solution.

STEP 1   Select **File > New** to open the New document dialog box. Under Preset, choose Photo, set the width and height to 5 inches, and click OK. You're going to recreate the arching text on the café sign in Figure 42-1.

Figure 42-1

STEP 2   Select the Ellipse tool (U), hold the Shift key, and draw out a large circle around 2.25 inches in diameter in the center of your file. Press T to select the Type tool, and on the Character panel choose a fun display font such as Greek Diner Inline TT, 45 pt with a hex value of #4f0f0f. Hover your cursor above the top edge of the circle shape and when the dotted lines around the cursor turn into a straight line (as if the cursor is surfing along the path), click once and type **PLANET** in all caps. If needed, use the Path Selection tool (A) to adjust the flow of your text along the path so that the text sits at the top of the arc.

STEP 3   Hide the visibility of the shape layer, select the text layer, and press Ctrl+J/⌘+J to duplicate the layer. Double-click the duplicate layer's thumbnail and replace the selected text with the word **MOCHA** in all caps. Use the Path Selection tool (A) to reposition the text along the bottom inside edge of the path, as illustrated in Figure 42-2.

 Figure 42-2

STEP 4   Double-click the MOCHA layer's thumbnail to select all the text, and in the Character panel adjust the character's tracking to about 275 so that the letters are more evenly spaced. That looks better, but the baselines of both text layers are still flowing along the edge of your original shape, which doesn't look very good.

With the MOCHA layer selected, press Ctrl+T/⌘+T to add a Transform bounding box around your type. To scale the layer, Shift+Alt+drag/Shift+Option+drag the bounding box so that the top arc of MOCHA aligns with the top arc of PLANET, and then press Enter/Return to accept the transformation. Your layout should now match the example in Figure 42-3.

Figure 42-3

STEP 5 Use the logo artwork on its own for marketing, advertising, and promotion, or as part of a layout like the café sign. For example, you could put the logo on a bag of coffee beans, a t-shirt, or a coffee mug (see Figure 42-4).

Figure 42-4

To complete the café sign layout from Figure 42-1, use the Ellipse tool to draw a circle shape behind the text with a fill color of #ceb28d and a 30 px inside stroke in #4f0f0f. Find a stock art picture of a coffee mug, select its shape, press the Refine Edge button to smooth out the selection edges. From the selection, create a new Color Fill Adjustment layer filled with the same color as the text, #4f0f0f. Hide the mug stock art layer and add an Inner Glow style to the mug fill layer with the blending mode set to Multiply and the color set to #4f0f0f. Lastly, add some text (Est. 1923) and a textured wood background layer.

TECHNIQUE

43

EMULATING TYPE EXPLODING IN SPACE

THERE ARE SEVERAL different techniques out there that mimic the look of text exploding in space, but none of them seems to have all the right elements to give you the most realistic, movie-style effect. Here you'll find a combination of the best techniques—plus a few extra twists— rolled into one comprehensive tutorial. May the force be with you!

STEP 1   Select **File** > **New** to open the New document dialog box. Under Preset choose Photo, set the width to 6 inches, the height to 3 inches, and click OK. Press D to reset the foreground and background colors, and then select **Edit** > **Fill** to fill the layer with the foreground color (Black).

STEP 2   Press T to select the Type tool, and on the Character panel choose a thick display font such as Gill Sans Ultra Bold, 30 pt with a bright purple hex value of #791097. Now type in the words **TRUST THE FORCE** in all capital letters.

STEP 3   Select the Background layer and press Shift+Ctrl+N/Shift⌘+N to create a new layer above it. Grab the Lasso tool (L) and draw a wobbly cloud-shaped selection around the text, as illustrated in Figure 43-1.

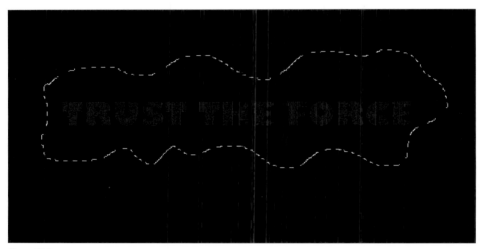

Figure 43-1

Press the Refine Edge button on the Control bar, adjust the Edge Feather to 32 px in the dialog box and click OK. Now select **Filter** > **Render** > **Clouds** and press Ctrl+D/⌘+D to deselect. Rename Layer 1 **Clouds**.

STEP 4   Duplicate (Ctrl+J/⌘+J) the Clouds layer and set the duplicate layer's blending mode to Pin Light. Now duplicate the Pin Light Clouds layer, change the blending mode to Luminosity, set the opacity to 20%, and select **Filter** > **Pixelate** > **Pointillize**. Set the cell size to 5 and click OK. You now have a nice, white gaseous nebula cloud behind your text.

STEP 5   Click the Levels icon on the Adjustments panel to create a new Levels adjustment layer. From the RGB menu, select Red and adjust the black histogram slider to about 87, so that the outer edges of your nebula cloud turn from white to a deep aquamarine blue. Cool.

STEP 6   Select the Type layer and choose **Layers** > **Rasterize** > **Type**. To create the illusion of exploding text, you're going to use your Lasso tool (L) to rope around different parts of the lettering and nudge them away from their starting points. Make an uneven selection around the top of a couple of letters, position your cursor inside the selection, and Ctrl+drag/⌘+drag the piece slightly away from the rest.

Repeat this process to blow up the letters as if they are bursting out or breaking up from the center of the image, as illustrated in Figure 43-2.

Figure 43-2

STEP 7   Next, you explode the type. Duplicate (Ctrl+J/⌘+J) the type layer and select **Filter** > **Blur** > **Radial Blur**. In the dialog box, set the amount to 65, the method to Zoom, and the quality to Best, and then click OK. Duplicate this layer twice more.

Change the top text layer's blending mode to Dissolve and lower the opacity to 50%.

In the Color panel, adjust the foreground color to a bright yellowish white with a hex value of #f5f5cc. Click the Lock Transparent Pixels icon on the Layers panel and select **Edit** > **Fill** to fill this layer with the foreground color.

STEP 8   Select the text layer copy directly below the one you just edited. Set the foreground color to a bright orange with a hex value of #dda41a.

Click the Lock Transparent Pixels icon on the Layers panel and select **Edit** > **Fill** to fill this layer with the foreground color.

Select the text layer directly below that and repeat the Lock and Fill process to fill the layer with a hex value of # 8d1878.

STEP 9   Reposition the original text layer to the top of the Layers panel, choose **Layer > Layer Style > Inner Shadow**, and then set the blending mode to Multiply, the color to #000000, the distance to 6 px, and the size to 1 px. Add a Bevel and Emboss style and set the style to Inner Bevel, the technique to Chisel Hard, the depth to 200%, the size to 6 px, the angle to 120°, and the altitude to 30°. Click OK.

To amplify the explosion effect, use the Transform Scale tool to slightly enlarge the duplicate text layers.

STEP 10   Last come some final lighting effects. Select the original text layer and choose **Filter > Render > Lens Flare**. Select the Movie Prime Lens type, set the brightness to 76%, and position the tiny + icon in the preview pane between the letter T and H in *The*. Press OK.

Create a new layer and position it directly beneath the original text layer. Set the blending mode to Dissolve and the opacity to 20%. Press D to reset the colors and D to put white in the foreground. Now press B to select the Brush tool, choose a large star-shaped brush, and set the size to about 900 px. Click a few times to set down clusters of scattered pixels.

Now select the Eraser tool, choose a large 900 px soft-edged brush and gently erase any solid clusters. Remember, you're going for a spacey explody effect, so trust your instincts. If you like this effect, repeat on another layer using yellow instead of white. Figure 43-3 shows the finished product.

Figure 43-3

TECHNIQUE 44

CLIPPING POSTERIZED PICTURES WITH TEXT

WHAT DO YOU get when you cross a few parts of a posterized photo with a block of text? A really cool and grungy, posterized, text-picture effect that looks great on postcards, business cards, posters, print ads, video graphics, and Websites. In this chapter, you'll learn how to quickly convert your photos into posterized layers, colorize them, and then clip them with text.

STEP 1   Select **File > New** to open the New document dialog box. Under Preset choose Photo, set the width and height to 5 inches, and click OK.

STEP 2   Paste a copy of a hamburger photo or some other object into the center of your file. Choose **Select > Color Range** to open the Color Range dialog box, and from the Select menu choose Midtones. Click OK. Press Shift+Ctrl+N/Shift+⌘+N to create a new layer, and then select **Edit > Fill**, and either select 50% Gray from the Use menu or choose Color and select a color such as #c48839 from the Color dialog box.

Reselect the hamburger layer, choose **Select > Color Range** to open the Color Range dialog box again, and this time choose Shadows from the Select menu and click OK. Press Shift+Ctrl+N/Shift+⌘+N to create a new layer, select **Edit > Fill**, and either select Black from the Use menu or choose Color and pick a color such as #3c2406 from the Color dialog box.

Hide the visibility of the original hamburger layer and select the midtones fill layer in the Layers panel. Your file should now look somewhat like the picture in Figure 44-1.

Figure 44-1

STEP 3 Press T to select the Type tool, choose a bold, casual body font such as Bell Gothic Std Bold with the size set to 12 pt, the alignment to Center, and the color to #3b2406. Click and drag out a text frame across the entire span of your hamburger, type or paste in enough text to cover the entire hamburger image, and then press Enter/Return. For example, you could type in the ingredients and instructions for a hamburger recipe, as shown in Figure 44-2.

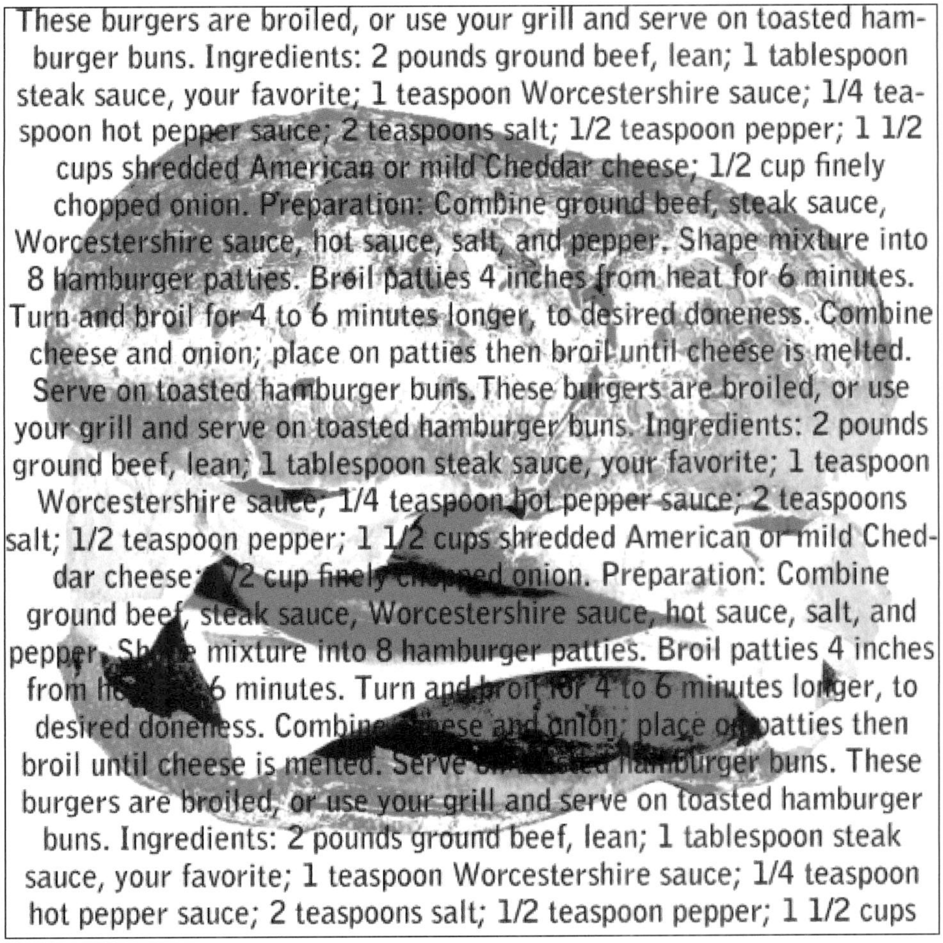

These burgers are broiled, or use your grill and serve on toasted hamburger buns. Ingredients: 2 pounds ground beef, lean; 1 tablespoon steak sauce, your favorite; 1 teaspoon Worcestershire sauce; 1/4 teaspoon hot pepper sauce; 2 teaspoons salt; 1/2 teaspoon pepper; 1 1/2 cups shredded American or mild Cheddar cheese; 1/2 cup finely chopped onion. Preparation: Combine ground beef, steak sauce, Worcestershire sauce, hot sauce, salt, and pepper. Shape mixture into 8 hamburger patties. Broil patties 4 inches from heat for 6 minutes. Turn and broil for 4 to 6 minutes longer, to desired doneness. Combine cheese and onion; place on patties then broil until cheese is melted. Serve on toasted hamburger buns. These burgers are broiled, or use your grill and serve on toasted hamburger buns. Ingredients: 2 pounds ground beef, lean; 1 tablespoon steak sauce, your favorite; 1 teaspoon Worcestershire sauce; 1/4 teaspoon hot pepper sauce; 2 teaspoons salt; 1/2 teaspoon pepper; 1 1/2 cups shredded American or mild Cheddar cheese; 1/2 cup finely chopped onion. Preparation: Combine ground beef, steak sauce, Worcestershire sauce, hot sauce, salt, and pepper. Shape mixture into 8 hamburger patties. Broil patties 4 inches from heat for 6 minutes. Turn and broil for 4 to 6 minutes longer, to desired doneness. Combine cheese and onion; place on patties then broil until cheese is melted. Serve on toasted hamburger buns. These burgers are broiled, or use your grill and serve on toasted hamburger buns. Ingredients: 2 pounds ground beef, lean; 1 tablespoon steak sauce, your favorite; 1 teaspoon Worcestershire sauce; 1/4 teaspoon hot pepper sauce; 2 teaspoons salt; 1/2 teaspoon pepper; 1 1/2 cups

Figure 44-2

STEP 4 Choose **Edit > Transform > Rotate** and rotate your text layer about 15° counterclockwise, and then press Enter/Return. To create a clipping mask from your text in the shape of your midtones layer, press Alt+Ctrl+G/Option+⌘+G.

Feel free to play around with the color of the text layer to achieve different results. For instance, you may like the layout better after changing the color to white. Great! When you have the colors the way you like them, use your grungy posterized text hamburger in a fun layout like the one shown in Figure 44-3.

Figure 44-3

SIMULATING ENGRAVED TYPE

ENGRAVED TYPE IS pretty popular these days (especially on the Web), thanks in large part to Adobe's use of engraved lettering in their product logo icons. For example, take a look at the icon you just clicked to launch Photoshop. Engraved type can take on many different vibes, depending on the font you choose and the surface graphic you embed the graved type into. Here you learn how to use Photoshop to carve into stone.

STEP 1   Select **File** > **New** to open the New document dialog box. Under Preset choose Photo, set the width to 7 inches, the height to 6 inches, and then click OK.

Open a second file that contains an image of a stone background texture, copy it, paste it into your file, and then close the original texture file.

INTERNET HINT: To find a suitable stone background texture for this technique, visit http://www.smashingmagazine.com/2009/02/06/100-beautiful-free-textures/.

STEP 2   For the type layer, use a bold, old-timey western font such as the wonderful and free Pointedly Mad font designed by Rich Gast. Visit http://www.greywolfwebworks.com to download and install a copy of the font on your computer. If Photoshop is open during the install, close and reopen it to gain access to the newly installed font.

Press T to select the Type tool, set the font to Pointedly Mad, the size to 50 pt, the alignment to Center, and the color to Black. Type in a few lines of text and adjust the size of the different lines as needed. Your layout should look something like Figure 45-1.

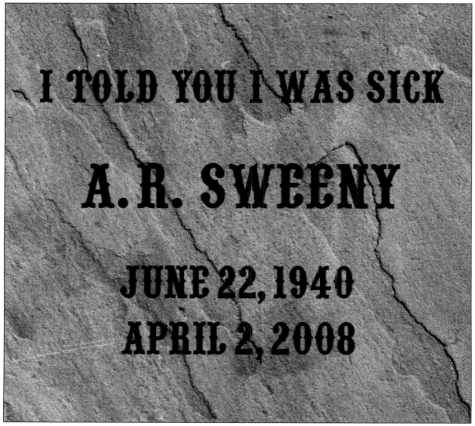

Figure 45-1

STEP 3   Ctrl+click/⌘+click the type layer's thumbnail to select the shapes of the letters, hide the visibility of the type layer, and click the Levels icon on the Adjustments panel. Adjust the bottom White Output levels slider from 255 to about 160 to darken the letters within the levels adjustment mask.

> HINT: To darken the selection, make sure you adjust the white Output levels slider toward the bottom of the panel rather than the white Histogram slider. If you accidently adjust the white Histogram levels slider from 255 to 160, your text will lighten rather than darken. Leave the Histogram sliders alone and only adjust the Output levels.

STEP 4   Click the Add Layer Style button at the bottom of the Layers panel, and apply Bevel and Emboss style. Set the style to Outer Bevel, the technique to Chisel Hard, the depth to 100%, the size to 2 px, the angle to 68°, the altitude to 30°, the highlight mode to 98%, and the shadow mode to 94%.

Don't close the Layer Styles dialog box just yet. You're going to add a few more styles.

STEP 5   Add the Drop Shadow style and set the blending mode to Overlay, the distance to 5 px, and the size to 21 px. Add the Inner Shadow style and set the distance to 5 px and the size to 6 px. To enhance the shadow, add an Inner Glow style and set the color to black, the blending mode to Color Burn, the opacity to 22%, and the size to 2 px. Now you can click OK to close the Layer Styles dialog box. Figure 45-2 shows you the finished effect.

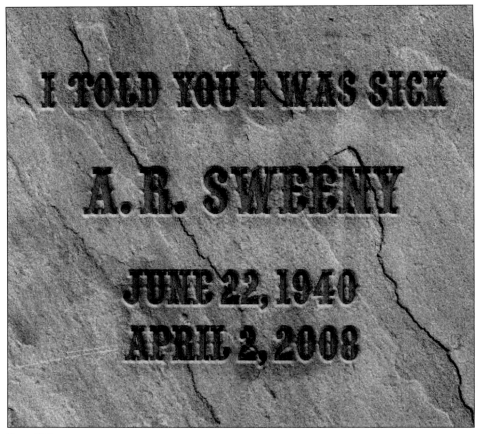

Figure 45-2

TECHNIQUE

46

PHOTO MASKING WITH TYPE

THE HORIZONTAL TYPE Mask tool is great for creating masks of photos and other objects in the shapes of letters, but it lacks one key element to make it truly useful—editability. With the Type Mask tool, once you press Enter and switch to another tool, you can't reposition your type atop a photo, and you certainly can't edit the text. Happily, Photoshop provides an alternate way to create masked type with fully editable text.

STEP 1   To illustrate how this technique works, you're going to create a promotional postcard. Select **File > New** to open the New document dialog box. Under Preset, choose Photo, set the width to 8.5 inches, the height to 6 inches, and then click OK.

Open a second file that contains an image of an interesting background texture, copy the entire image, close the file, and paste it into your first document.

> *INTERNET HINT: You can find some wonderful free background textures at http:// www.smashingmagazine.com/texture-gallery-stone-walls-brick/.*

STEP 2   Press T to select the Type tool, set the font to Impact, the size to 112 pt, the leading to 112 pt, the alignment to Center, and the color to Black. Type the word **Minimalism** three times on three lines and use the Move tool to position the type layer in the center of the document, as illustrated in Figure 46-1.

Figure 46-1

STEP 3   In the Layers panel, move the type layer below the background texture layer so you can no longer see your text. Now, hold down the Alt/Option key and hover your cursor right above the dividing line between these two layers. When your cursor turns from a hand to the Clipping Mask symbol (which looks like two overlapping circles), click the divider. This clips the background image with the shape of the letters on the text layer, as seen in Figure 46-2.

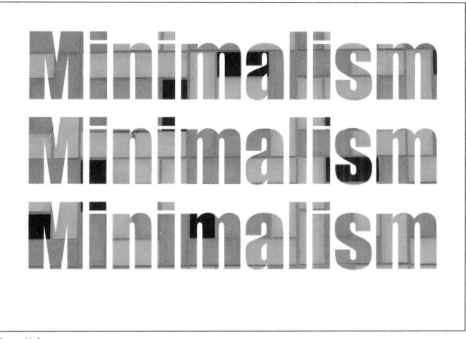

Figure 46-2

HINT: You can also create a clipping mask from a selected layer by pressing Ctrl+Alt+G/⌘+Option+G or selecting Layer > Create Clipping Mask.

STEP 4   That's good, but the text would look better in all caps. Double-click the text layer's thumbnail to reselect all the text and replace the type with three rows of the word **MINIMAL-ISM** in all caps. Much better.

STEP 5   Now add some Layer Styles to the text layer. Click the Add Layer Style button at the bottom of the Layers panel and choose Drop Shadow. Set the distance to 18 px and the size to 7 px. Add the Inner Shadow style and set the distance to 5 px and the size to 6 px. Next, add the Stroke style, set the color to #662d28 (or a dark color sampled from your background texture image), the size to 3 px, and click OK.

STEP 6   To finish the postcard layout, select the white background layer, press T to select the Type tool, set the font to Impact, the size to 24 pt, the tracking to -2, the alignment to Center, and the color to Black. Type the words (in all caps) **AMERICAN MINIMALISM 1960s-1970s AT THE PARK MUSEUM**. Use the Move tool to position this text evenly below the other type layer, as illustrated in Figure 46-3, and you're done.

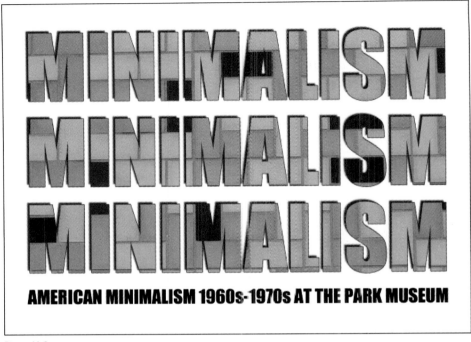

Figure 46-3

TECHNIQUE 47

MAKING GLASS TEXT

OVER THE CENTURIES, glass has been used both indoors and out for a variety of things, such as vases, vessels, and sculptures; windows, walls, and doors; trophies, awards, signs, and trinkets; table tops, glasses, and tableware; and even tiles and interior dividers. Glass can be etched, blown, stained, poured, and carved, and now, with Photoshop, you can make lettering and other objects appear as if they, too, are made of carved glass.

STEP 1   Select **File > New** to open the New document dialog box. Under Preset, choose Web, set the width to 800, the height to 480, and click OK.

STEP 2   Set your foreground color to #323a24 and your background color to #6c6e1d. Then select the Rectangular Marquee tool (M) and drag a horizontal rectangular selection across the bottom quarter of the window. Click the Create New Fill or Adjustment Layer icon at the bottom of the Layers panel, select Gradient, and when the Gradient Fill dialog box opens, select the Foreground to Background option from the Gradient menu, set the angle to 0°, and click OK.

Now set your background color to #f1f3dc, press X to flip the Background to the Foreground, select the Rectangular Marquee tool (M) and drag a horizontal rectangular selection across the top three-quarters of the window. Click the Create New Fill or Adjustment Layer icon at the bottom of the Layers panel, and then select Gradient. When the Gradient Fill dialog box opens, select the Foreground to Background option from the Gradient menu, set the angle to 145°, and click OK.

STEP 3   Press T to select the Type tool, set the font to Impact, the size to 200 pt, and the color to black. Type the word **DYNASTY** in all caps and use the Move tool to position the type layer near the center of the document, as illustrated in Figure 47-1.

Figure 47-1

STEP 4   To give the text that shiny, carved-from-glass look, you need to add several Layer Styles. Click the Add Layer Style button at the bottom of the Layers panel and choose Bevel and Emboss. Set the style to Inner Bevel, the size to 22 px, the soften to 3 px, the altitude to 66°, the highlight mode to 98%, and the shadow mode to Color Burn at 30%. Select Cone – Inverted from the Contour menu and click the Anti-aliased checkbox.

Next, click the Blending Options at the top of the dialog box, set the fill opacity to 20%, and enable the Blend Interior Effects as a Group checkbox.

Now, apply a drop shadow. Lower the opacity to 65% and set the distance to 18 px and the size to 15 px. Add the Inner Shadow style, raise the opacity to 78%, change the color to #444444, set the distance to 7 px, the choke to 14%, and the size to 20 px.

Next, add the Outer Glow style, set the color to #c8c8c8, the opacity to 45%, and the size to 12 px. Then click OK. Figure 47-2 shows how the effect looks so far.

Figure 47-2

STEP 5   To add a bit more shine, Ctrl+click/⌘+click the text layer thumbnail to select the letter shapes. With your Elliptical Marquee tool (M) selected, hold down the Alt/Option key and deselect the lower half of the letters in a sloping circular loop. Click the Levels icon on the Adjustments panel and move the white point marker from 255 to 178. Then adjust the Levels Adjustment Layer's opacity to 30%.

STEP 6   For a final hint of sparkle, select the Polygon Shape tool (U), click the Geometry Options menu (next to the blobby shape) on the Options bar, check the Star option and set the Indent Sides By to 99%. Drag out a pointy star shape on the shiniest area at the top of the D. This creates a Shape layer. To add additional shapes to this same layer, click the Add to Shape Area icon on the Options bar and continue dragging out different sized star shapes across the shiniest parts of a few more letters.

STEP 7   Now that you've created a carved glass style, you can apply it to any other shape or text layer by choosing Copy Layer Style (and then Paste Layer Style) from your glass text layer's context menu, as illustrated in Figure 47-3.

Figure 47-3

TECHNIQUE

48

USING KNOCKOUT SHAPES

A *KNOCKOUT IS* a wonderfully rich and layered way to work with shapes, images, and text. Essentially, with a knockout you can punch through one layer with a shape or text to reveal objects and images on the underlying background layer. You really have to try this and see it yourself to truly understand how creative you can be with this technique.

The project outlined here requires two same-sized photographs and one text layer. Once you get to the end of the exercise, you can try replacing the image layers with shape and text layers to create some amazing, unique effects.

STEP 1   Begin by opening a 300 dpi photographic image file in your workspace. The photograph should be the only layer in the Photoshop file and thus be a locked background layer. This background layer will become the image revealed through the shape or text on the top-most layer. To convert a regular layer into a background layer, choose **Layer > New > Background From Layer**.

STEP 2   Open a second file of another 300 dpi photographic image, copy it and close the file, and then paste the copied image into your first document. The pasted image should be a regular layer.

STEP 3   Press T to select the Type tool, choose a thick, fun display font such as Budmo Jiggler with the size and leading set to 160 pt, the alignment to Center, and the color to #e38b00. Click in the center of the file and type in any two words on two lines, such as **HONEY BEES**, as shown in Figure 48-1.

Figure 48-1

STEP 4   To make your text stand out from the photo image, click the Add Layer Style button at the bottom of the Layers panel and apply the Bevel and Emboss style. Set the style to Outer Bevel, the depth to 145%, and the size to 9 px. To further define the letters, add a Stroke style and set the size to 10 px, the opacity to 80%, and the color to #c56a02.

For this effect to work properly, stack your layers so that knockout shape/text layer is on top, the punch-through layer is in the middle, and the locked background layer is at the bottom. If you need to adjust the order of your layers, or would rather use different photos, shapes, or text, change them now before proceeding.

STEP 5   Select the text layer, click the Add a Layer Style icon at the bottom of the Layers panel, and choose Blending Options. When the dialog box opens, select Deep from the Knockout menu. This knocks out the selected layer's shape through to the background. In the Advanced Blending section, lower the fill opacity to 0% to reveal the locked background layer's image in the shape of your text!

> HINT: For an alternate effect, reset the fill opacity to 100% and choose one of the blending modes from the General Blending section, such as Soft Light or Linear Burn.

Click OK and you're done. Figure 48-2 shows an example of a finished knockout effect.

Figure 48-2

TECHNIQUE

49

MAKING TEXT WITH 3D PERSPECTIVE

BEFORE PHOTOSHOP CS5'S advanced 3D tools came along, the only way to create text with a 3D perspective in Photoshop was to fake it. Barring that, the only other option was to buy an expensive plug-in or create 3D text with another program. Here you'll learn the secret of using Photoshop to create text that gives the illusion of 3D perspective.

STEP 1   Select **File** > **New** to open the New document dialog box. Under Preset, choose Photo, set the width to 6.15 inches, the height to 4 inches, and click OK.

STEP 2   Press T to select the Type tool, choose a bold, assertive display font such as Antigoni Bd Bold with the size set to 60 pt, the alignment to Center, and the color to black. Click in the center of the file and in all capital letters type the words **NEW FORMULA**.

STEP 3   Select **Layer** > **Rasterize** > **Type** to rasterize the text layer. Then select **Edit** > **Transform** > **Perspective** to call up the transformation bounding box around your letters. Click and drag the bottom-left marker downwards a few inches to make the left-most letter larger, and then click and drag the center right marker downwards just a bit so that the bounding box line spanning across the top edge of all the letters is perfectly horizontal, as shown in Figure 49-1. When you have the transformation the way you want it, press Enter/ Return.

198

Figure 49-1

STEP 4   Here's a great keyboard shortcut: Press Alt+←/Option+← to automatically duplicate and nudge your text 1 px to the left. Click the Lock Transparent Pixels icon at the top of the Layers panel, set the Foreground color to #648825, and press Shift+F5 to fill the layer with the foreground color.

> HINT: *If this keyboard shortcut doesn't perform this command on your computer with your particular version of Photoshop, duplicate the layer by pressing Ctrl+J/ ⌘+J and then nudge the duplicate layer 1 px to the left by pressing the ← key on your keyboard.*

STEP 5   Select your black rasterized text layer and press Alt+←/Option+← 20 times. With the top-most duplicate type layer selected, Shift+click the bottom-most black type layer to select it and all the layers in between, and then press Ctrl+E/⌘+E to merge the selected layers.

STEP 6   To make the front of the lettering pop, select the green text layer, click the Add Layer Style button at the bottom of the Layers panel, and apply Bevel and Emboss style. Set the style to Inner Bevel, the depth to 45%, the size to 18 px, the angle to 3°, and the altitude to 45°. Then click OK to close the dialog box.

Figure 49-2 shows the finished text used in an advertising layout. If desired, you can further enhance the fake 3D text effect by adding one or more of the following layer styles:

- To give the illusion of 3D text mounted on a wall, add a Drop Shadow effect with the angle set to 24°, the distance set to 10 px, and the size set to 10 px.

- To add texture to the front of your letters, paste a textured image into your file and position it above the green text layer. With the texture layer selected, Ctrl+click/⌘+click the green text layer's thumbnail to select letter shapes, press Shift+Ctrl+I/Shift+⌘−I to inverse the selection, and press Backspace/Delete to delete. Adjust the blending mode of the textured layer to Overlay, Soft Light, Hard Light, or Pin Light.

- To add shading to the sides of the 3D letters, add a Gradient Overlay style with the opacity set between 25%–65%. Use the default (black to white) or choose one of the preset gradients.

199

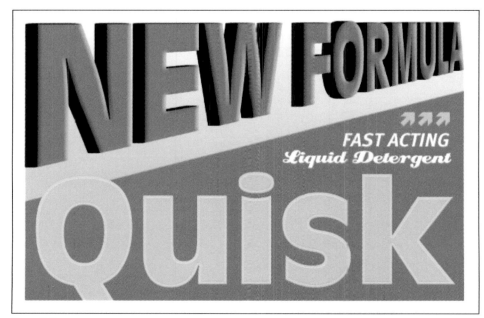

Figure 49-2

CREATING WORN AND WEATHERED TEXT

ONE OF THE best ways to add depth, texture, and visual interest to your print, video, and Web layouts is to create the illusion of worn, grungy, distressed, and weathered text. Although you could use a premade distressed font in your work, you'll likely run the risk of having repeating distress marks when the same letters are used.

To avoid having your distressed text look patterned, use this new Photoshop technique. This effect not only provides a hint of dimensionality to flat artwork, but it also gives your work a sense of authority and legitimacy by making it seem older, seasoned, and perhaps even wiser.

STEP 1   Select **File > New** to open the New document dialog box. Under Preset choose Photo, set the width and height to 5 inches, and click OK.

STEP 2   Press T to select the Type tool, choose a thick, fun display font with the size set to 65 pt, the alignment to Center, and the color to #72210f. Click in the center of the file and type the words **PRODUCT OF INDIA**. Adjust the font size and font face for each word as needed.

Select the Ellipse tool (U) and drag a circle across the center of the page to cover the text. Click the Add a Layer Style button at the bottom of the Layers panel and add a 30 px outside stroke with the same color, #72210f, then click OK. Adjust the circle shape's fill to 0%.

Select the Custom Shape tool (U), click on the Custom Shape Picker drop-down menu on the Control panel, click the Pattern pop-up panel menu to view the list of available shape libraries and select Ornaments. Now scroll down in the Custom Shape Picker menu and select the design called Ornament 6. Shift+drag to create a small ornament shape within the circle above the text. Repeat to add a second ornament shape within the circle below the text. If your shape layers include the same stroke style as the circle, disable or delete the style. Your file should now look like the example in Figure 50-1.

Figure 50-1

STEP 3   With the text layer selected, Shift+click the bottom shape layer to select it and all the layers in between (do not include the locked background layer), and then press and hold Alt/Option as you select Merge Layers from the Layers panel menu to create a new layer with a merged copy of all the selected layers.

HINT: If you're having trouble creating a merged copy of the selected layers using the Merge Layers command, be sure you are pressing and holding the Alt/Option key both before you access the Layers panel menu and while you select the Merge Layers command.

With the new merged layer selected, hide the visibility of all the original layers, select **Edit > Transform > Rotate**, and rotate the image about 15° to the left.

50-2A shows how your artwork should look so far. Refer to the other images in this figure as you perform the remaining steps.

Figure 50-2

STEP 4   Open a second file that contains an image of wall background texture (visit http://www.smashingmagazine.com/2009/02/06/100-beautiful-free-textures/), copy it, close it, and paste it into your file above the merged art layer. Scale the texture layer as needed to be slightly larger than the size of the merged art layer.

With the texture layer still selected, Ctrl+click/⌘+click the merged art layer's thumbnail to select the pixels, press Shift+Ctrl+I/Shift+⌘+I to inverse the selection, and press Backspace/Delete to cut the wall texture layer into the shape of the merged art layer (see Figure 50-2B).

Click the Threshold button on the Adjustments panel and adjust the threshold level slider from 128 to around 173 so that the texture is mostly black with a few areas that look worn and weathered (see Figure 50-2C).

With the Threshold adjustment layer selected, Shift+click to select the wall texture shape layer and then hide the Threshold adjustment and wall shape layers in the Layers panel. Then press and hold Alt/Option as you select Merge Layers from the Layers panel menu to create a new layer with a merged copy.

STEP 5   To create your final artwork, move this new merged layer above the original art layer, adjust the blending mode of this new layer to Lighten, Shift+click to select the art layer, and press and hold Alt/Option as you select Merge Layers from the Layers panel menu to create a new layer with a merged copy (see Figure 50-2D).

Use your final artwork on its own as a graphic text treatment or as an element within a larger layout, as shown on the product label in Figure 50-3.

Figure 50-3

IV STUDIO AND COMMERCIAL EFFECTS

MAKING MAGICAL REFLECTED SURFACES

PROFESSIONAL STUDIO PHOTOGRAPHERS often set up product shots using a display table with one or two different colored Plexiglas sheets rather than using glass and mirrors. The Plexiglas is used as a support and a smooth, lightweight, reflective surface. Plexiglas has strength, opacity, durability, and it is easy to clean. Not only that, but you can bend it to create continuous colored slopes, illuminate it from below, and throw colored light on it from any direction.

Reflections give the illusion of depth and dimension, especially when combined with flat objects and text. With Photoshop, you can apply a mock Plexiglas reflective effect to your artwork in just a few simple steps.

STEP 1 Select **File** > **New** to open the New document dialog box. From Preset choose Photo. Set the width to 7 inches, the height to 10 inches, and click OK.

STEP 2 You're going to create the reflective surface menu design shown in Figure 51-1, starting with the text. To add the shiny style text at the top of the menu, follow the steps in Technique #41, "Creating Shiny Plastic Text."

Figure 51-1

To add the word *Menu* along the bottom, select the Type tool (T), choose a fancy cursive font with the size set to 45 pt, the alignment to Center, and the color to black, and then click near the bottom of the file and type the word **Menu**.

STEP 3   Select **File > Place** to open the Place dialog box. Browse to and select a picture of a burger (or some other food item), click the Place button, and then press Enter/Return to accept the artwork as a Vector Smart Object layer.

If your placed image has a white matte, select **Layer > Rasterize > Smart Object** to rasterize the layer, use the Magic Wand tool (W) to select the matte, and press Delete/Backspace to delete it.

Use the Move tool (V) to position the burger in the center of the file below the text. To give the burger a subtle defined edge, click the Add Layer Style button at the bottom of the Layers panel and select Outer Glow. Set the blending mode to Multiply, the color to #ac7848, and the size to 13 px. Then click OK to close the dialog box.

So far, so good. Figure 51-2 shows what your menu layout should look like at this stage.

STEP 4   Ctrl+click/⌘+click the hamburger layer's thumbnail to select the pixels, press Ctrl+C/⌘+C to copy, then press Ctrl+V/⌘+V to paste the copy onto a new layer. Select **Edit > Transform > Flip Vertical**, and use the Move tool (V) to move the upside-down burger to just below the bottom edge of the right side up burger. Now, right+click/Ctrl+click the upside down layer and choose Clear Layer Style from the layer's context menu, then move the upside down layer below the normal hamburger layer in the Layers panel.

STEP 5   Press D to reset the foreground and background colors, press X to put white on top, press G to select the Gradient tool, and on the Options bar, choose Foreground to Transparent from the Gradient menu and select Linear Gradient as the gradient type.

Figure 51-2

Drag a gradient from the bottom edge of the menu layout to the center of the normal hamburger layer. Getting your reflection just right might take a few more passes with the Gradient tool. Look at Figure 51-3 for guidance. If you go too far, use the History panel to undo and retry until you get your gradient just right.

Figure 51-3

STEP 6 For the final touches on the menu (seen in Figure 51-1), add a couple of background gradients. Select the background layer at the bottom of the Layers panel, press Shift+Ctrl+N/Shift+⌘+N to create a new blank layer, and use the Rectangular Marquee tool (M) to select the top third of the layout. Set the foreground color to #ffe482, press G to select the Gradient tool, and drag a gradient from the top to the bottom of the selection.

Press Shift+Ctrl+N/Shift+⌘+N to create another new blank layer, and use the Rectangular Marquee tool (M) to select a rectangular shape that spans from the middle of the hamburger to the bottom of the layout. Set the foreground color to #6f9f0d, press G to select the Gradient tool, and drag a gradient from the top to the bottom of the selection.

Bon Appétit!

52

TECHNIQUE

MAKING DREAM-LIKE PHOTO COMPOSITES

PHOTOSHOP CELEBRATED ITS 20th anniversary in 2010, and although the program's roots are in traditional photography, the fact that we can use the software to digitally construct and manipulate images has completely changed the way we think about truth in photographs. Fantasy images can now be seen everywhere we look—in advertising, television, movies, videos, games, and art.

In this technique, you will learn how to create a dream-like fantasy image using photo-compositing techniques such as blur and photo filters, smudging, adjustment layers with different blending modes, and lens flares. All you need to begin are a couple of stock images: one scene with dramatic clouds and another of a landscape that contains a focal point such as a person, animal, or product.

STEP 1 Select **File > New** to open the New document dialog box. From Preset choose Photo, choose Landscape, 8×10 as the size, and click OK. If you prefer to work with a different layout, select **Image > Image Size** to adjust the document dimensions and resolution.

Open both of your starting images (clouds and landscape/subject) and paste them into your document, one on each layer, with the clouds above the landscape layer. Figure 52-1 shows the two starting images used in this tutorial alongside the final fantasy composite image.

Figure 52-1

STEP 2 Using your Magic Wand (W) and other selection tools as needed, make a selection in your landscape layer of everything you want to be in the final image (such as the foreground, subject, and part of the landscape), and select **Layer > New Layer Via Copy**. Move this new layer above the clouds layer within the Layers panel.

Select your clouds layer in the Layers panel, and use the selection tools to select and delete any non-cloud parts of the image. If needed, adjust the position of the clouds layer so that it overlaps the landscape layer in a natural way. You should now have three layers: the original landscape on bottom, a clouds layer in the center, and the copied landscape layer on top, as illustrated in Figure 52-2.

Figure 52-2

STEP 3 To make your clouds darker and more dramatic, select the clouds layer, click the Levels icon on the Adjustments panel, and adjust the histogram sliders so that the blacks and midtones are darker than normal. For example, in the clouds image in Figure 52-2, the black point was set to 19, the gray point was set to 0.25, and the white point was set to 218.

STEP 4 Next, visually blend the two images together with adjustment layers. Select the copied landscape layer, click the Hue/Saturation icon on the Adjustments panel, and set the Saturation to -42.

Click the Return to Adjustment List icon (arrow) at the bottom of the Adjustments panel and click the Levels icon. Set the black point to 51, the gray point to 1.00, and the white point to 240.

Click the Return to Adjustment List icon (arrow) at the bottom of the Adjustments panel and click the Gradient Map icon. Double-click the Gradient bar to open the Gradient Editor dialog box. Click the black color stop at the bottom of the Gradient Editor bar and click the black color picker field to change the black to a bright yellow with the hex value of #f6c20f. Click OK to accept that color, and click OK again to close the Color Editor. Change the blending mode of the Gradient Map layer to Color Burn.

215

STEP 5   To give your foreground subject a dreamier quality, select your landscape copy layer and duplicate it by pressing Ctrl+J/⌘+J. With the duplicate layer selected, select **Filter > Blur > Gaussian Blur** to apply a blur with a 45 px radius, and then select **Filter > Sharpen > Sharpen Edges** to sharpen that layer back up a bit. Now set this layer's blending mode to Multiply. Figure 52-3 shows the image before (top) and after (bottom) adding the blur/sharpen layer.

Figure 52-3

STEP 6   Reselect the landscape copy layer, and use the Eraser tool (E) to erase away any distracting areas within the image and around the outer edges to help create a vignette effect. Next, use the Smudge tool around the outer edges of this layer to help tie all the environmental elements together. Smudging is especially helpful with edge areas such as hair, grass, and trees.

STEP 7   Now you'll add a little more atmospheric lighting. Select the clouds layer and click the Curves icon on the Adjustments panel. Click in the center of the curves histogram to add a gray point marker and then drag that marker downwards and to the left to darken the clouds. For example, you may want to set the output to 55 and the input to 87.

Select the mask thumbnail in the Curves adjustment layer and then select the Brush tool (B). Using a 200 px soft-edged brush, paint (with black) light streaks in the sky, as if the moon were shining rays of light through the clouds.

STEP 8   For a more surrealistic color scheme, select the blurred and sharpened landscape layer, click the Color Balance icon on the Adjustments layer, and adjust the color values for the shadows, midtones, and highlights to your liking. In this example, the following values are used:

- Shadows: Red -2, Green -5, Blue -5
- Midtones: Red -71, Green +1, Blue -10
- Highlights: Red +43, Green -2, Blue -72

Click the Return to Adjustment List icon (arrow) at the bottom of the Adjustments panel.

STEP 9   To warm up the entire scene, select the Gradient Map layer, press the Photo Filter icon on the Adjustments panel, select the Warming Filter (85), and adjust the density to 55%.

STEP 10   Finally, you'll add a lens flare to set a focal point in the image. Select the landscape copy layer, press Ctrl+J/⌘+J to duplicate it, and move the duplicate above the Color Balance layer in the Layers panel. Select **Filter > Render > Lens Flare** and, when the dialog box opens, position the Flare Mark (+) in the preview window at the desired focal point within the image. Set the Lens Type to 50–300 mm zoom, the brightness to 100%, and click OK. Figure 52-4 shows the example image before (top) and after (bottom) adding the lens flare, which really helps to soften up the overall dreamy quality of the composite image.

Figure 52-4

CREATING MOTION AT WARP SPEED

PHOTOSHOP HAS SEVERAL blur filters that you can apply to your images to give the illusion of realistic movement. Motion blur, for example, is the effect you see when a person uses a camera with a slow shutter speed to photograph a fast-moving person, animal, or object, like an action shot at a football game, a wild animal running through the savannah, or a speeding car on a racetrack. In addition to using blur filters to simulate natural movement, you can also use them to create the look of motion in outer space. This tutorial teaches you how to use motion blur along with several other filters to make a rocket blast through the cosmos.

STEP 1   Open a file in Photoshop of a simple photo of a toy spaceship, similar to the one shown in Figure 53-1. The resolution of this image will determine the size of your workspace. For instance, in the example image used here, the resolution is 300 ppi and the size is 3008×2000 px, or roughly 10×6.5 inches. Name this layer *original*.

Figure 53-1

STEP 2   Use the Quick Selection (W) and other selection tools as needed to select the toy shape, and then press the Refine Edge button on the Control bar. When the dialog box opens, set the smooth to 16, the feather to 3.0, and click OK. Press Ctrl+J/⌘+J to place a copy of the selection onto a new layer, then name that layer *spaceship*.

Ctrl+click/⌘+click the new spaceship layer's thumbnail in the Layers panel, press Shift+Ctrl+I/ Shift+⌘+I to inverse the selection, select the *original* layer, and then select **Filter > Blur > Motion Blur.** When the dialog box opens, set the angle to match the direction of the toy object, such as of -31°, set the distance to 400 px, and click OK. Press Ctrl+D/⌘+D to deselect.

STEP 3   With the spaceship layer selected, click the Add Layer Style button and apply an outer glow with the opacity set to 28% and the size set to 35 px. Click OK. This sets the toy layer slightly apart from the background layer as well as giving it a subtle aura of extreme heat.

STEP 4   To make it appear a bit more as if the toy is rocketing through space, as shown in Figure 53-2, select the spaceship layer and press Ctrl+J/⌘+J to create a duplicate of it. Rename the duplicate layer *spaceship blur* and position it below the spaceship layer in the Layers panel. With the spaceship blur layer selected, select **Filter > Blur > Motion Blur,** and when the dialog box opens, set the angle to match the direction of the toy object, such as -31°, set the distance to 400 px, and click OK.

Figure 53-2

STEP 5   Next you'll add a little atmosphere. Ctrl+click/⌘+click the spaceship layer's thumbnail, press Shift+Ctrl+I/Shift+⌘+I to inverse the selection, select the original layer, and click the Hue/Saturation icon on the Adjustments panel. Click the Colorize checkbox, set the hue slider to 207, the saturation to 46, and the lightness to -75.

To add clouds, press Ctrl+D/⌘+D to deselect, select the Hue/Saturation layer in the Layers panel, and press Ctrl+J/⌘+J to duplicate the layer. Rename this duplicate layer *clouds*, and then select **Filter > Render Clouds**. To make the clouds even cloudier, select **Filter > Render Difference Clouds** a few more times. Select **Filter > Noise > Add Noise** and set the Amount to 118% with a uniform distribution, then click OK. Lastly, change the blending mode of this layer to Hard Mix. Now the image is starting to look dark and moody!

STEP 6   To add more light and exhaust trails behind the spaceship, select the spaceship blur layer and press Shift+Ctrl+N/ Shift+⌘+N to create a new blank layer above it. Press B to select the Brush tool and with the foreground color set to #24ba99 and the brush size set to 250 px, paint three soft-edged strokes flowing away from the tail end of the toy into the distance. Then set the blending mode to Color Dodge.

STEP 7   To add stardust and stars to the scene, select the spaceship layer, and press Shift+Ctrl+N/ Shift+⌘+N to create a new blank layer above it. With a thick, soft-edged brush, dab a flew white blobs in the sky and change the blending mode to Soft Light. Press Shift+Ctrl+N/Shift+⌘+N again to create another new blank layer, and with the same brush, dab a flew more white blobs in the sky, only this time change the blending mode to Subtract. Create a third new blank layer and repeat with painting blobs, change the blending mode to Dissolve, and position this layer below the spaceship layer.

STEP 8   Finally, to make the spaceship look a little more futuristic, select the spaceship layer, press Ctrl+J/⌘+J to duplicate it, move the layer to the top of the Layers panel, and select **Filters > Stylize > Glowing Edges**. Set the edge width to 2, the edge brightness to 6, and the smoothness to 5. Click OK, and you're done. Figure 53-3 shows the final outer space scene.

Figure 53-3

TECHNIQUE
54

BUILDING MOCK STUDIO LIGHTING

WITH STOCK IMAGES, sometimes finding the right photograph is like searching for the proverbial needle in a haystack. Locating the right picture of a person or object is hard enough, but finding the subject in the right setting is nearly impossible unless you shoot the image yourself. Thankfully, there is a solution. With Photoshop, you can easily pull a subject from a plain stock image and move it into a scene so that it looks like your subject was photographed in a studio with professional studio lighting.

STEP 1   Start by opening a photo of a person or other object in Photoshop and use the Pen tool (P) to draw a tight, closed path around the outer edges of your subject, as illustrated in Figure 54-1. In the Path panel, select the Work Path layer, and press the Load Path as a Selection icon at the bottom of the panel. Press Shift+F6 to open the Feather Selection dialog box, enter a radius of **1 px**, and click OK. Now press Ctrl+J/⌘+J to place a copy of the selection onto a new layer.

Figure 54-1

STEP 2   To place the copied subject in a neutral setting, you need a neutral background. Select the original photo layer, press Shift+Ctrl+N/Shift+⌘+N to create a new blank layer above it, and select **Edit > Fill** to fill the layer with #8a8a8a.

STEP 3   Select the subject layer and use the Smudge tool to smooth out any rough or jagged edges and blend the subject into the neutral setting. This is especially helpful for fine, wispy areas like the hairline.

> HINT: If you'd like to work more non-destructively on your image, consider using the Refine Edges and Mask tools in addition to or instead of the Smudge tool.

If the subject needs color correction and tonal balancing, add a Curves or Levels Adjustment layer through the Adjustments panel. You may also want to increase the contrast slightly with a Brightness/Contrast Adjustment layer.

STEP 4   To create the mock studio lighting you need to add a few layers. Start by selecting the gray background layer and press Shift+Ctrl+N/ Shift+⌘+N twice to create two new blank layers. Select the bottom new layer and use the Gradient tool (G) to apply a black to transparent gradient from the top-left corner to the bottom-right corner, and then set the opacity of the layer to 80%. Select the top new layer, and then use the Gradient tool (G) to apply a white to transparent gradient from the bottom-left corner to the top-right, and set the opacity of this layer to 40%.

STEP 5   Add a floor by selecting the gray background layer and using the Rectangular Marquee tool (M) to select the bottom eighth of the document. Press Shift+Ctrl+N/ Shift+⌘+N to create another blank layer, set the foreground color to #343434, and press Shift+F5 to fill the selection with that foreground color. Select **Filter > Blur > Gaussian Blur**, set the radius to 45 px, and click OK. Then select a 250 px soft-edged brush with the opacity set to 95%, and blend the floor into the background by painting a few soft strokes across the edge.

STEP 6   Select the white to transparent gradient layer, press Shift+Ctrl+N/ Shift+⌘+N to create a new layer, adjust the opacity of the layer to 65%, and paint a blobby shadow directly below and to the left, behind the subject. If needed, apply the Gaussian Blur filter to soften the effect a bit more. Click the Hue/Saturation icon on the Adjustments panel to add a tint to the gray background. Set the hue to 70 (or another hue of your choice), the saturation to 25, and the lightness to +33. Your final image should look something like the example in Figure 54-2.

Figure 54-2

TECHNIQUE

55

ENHANCING EDITORIALS WITH PATTERNS

EDITORIAL ADVERTISEMENTS TAKE on many different guises, depending on what product or service you are marketing. Often, editorials use a photograph of a person to illustrate the effectiveness of the product or service. One of the most useful ways to make that person stand out from the background is to employ the use of patterns, which can go on top of as well as behind the subject.

STEP 1   Select **File** > **New** to open the New document dialog box. Under Preset, choose Photo and from Pixel Dimensions set the width to 900 px, the height to 900 px, and click OK.

STEP 2   Open a separate file that contains an image of a person and make a selection of that person using any of the selection tools, quick mask, or the Pen tool. When you have the person selected, choose **Select** > **Modify** > **Feather** to open the Feather Selection dialog box, enter a radius of **1 px**, and click OK. Now press Ctrl+C/⌘+C to copy the selection and then close the person file. Return to your new blank file and press Ctrl+V/⌘+V to paste the image onto a new layer, as shown in Figure 55-1.

Figure 55-1

STEP 3   For a pattern, you can use one of the presets that come with Photoshop, download and install patterns from a third-party provider, or create your own, as you learned in Technique #2.

To create a lined pattern, select **File > New** to open the New document dialog box, and from Preset choose Web, from Pixel Dimensions set the width and height to 3 px, and click OK. Using the Pencil tool (B), draw a 1 px black stripe down the center of the document. Press Ctrl+A/⌘+A to select all, and then choose **Edit > Define Pattern**. When the Pattern Name dialog box appears, enter **Stripes** as the name of your new pattern and click OK. Then close the file without saving.

STEP 4   Ctrl+click/⌘+click the person layer's thumbnail to select the shape, click the Create New Fill or Adjustment Layer button at the bottom of the Layers panel, and choose Pattern. The Pattern Fill dialog box appears displaying your new stripes pattern. If needed, adjust the scale, and then click OK. Then change the blending mode to Soft Light.

STEP 5   If you'd like to tint the image with a slight uniform tone, Ctrl+click/⌘+click the Pattern Fill layer's thumbnail, click the Hue/Saturation icon on the Adjustments panel, and set the hue to 30, the saturation to 5, and the lightness to 0.

STEP 6   For the background, you'll create an undulating, silky fabric background from scratch. Select the background layer and press Shift+Ctrl+N/Shift+⌘+N to create a new blank layer above it. Press D to reset the colors, press G to select the Gradient tool, and on the Options bar make sure that the gradient goes from foreground to background, the style is set to Linear, the mode is set to Difference, and the opacity is set to 60%.

Using the Gradient tool, drag the cursor diagonally across the layer and release the mouse. Repeat this action about 20–30 more times, going from top to bottom and bottom to top in the same diagonal direction, to build the folds in the fabric. Then, to add color, click the Color Balance icon on the Adjustments panel and adjust the color sliders for the shadows, midtones, and highlights to your liking. Figure 55-2 shows the final image with the lined pattern overlay and a silky fabric background.

Figure 55-2

TECHNIQUE

56

MELTING OBJECTS

THE MOST EYE-CATCHING images used today in advertising and marketing often include some kind of visual gimmick to attract viewers, such as fire, ice, glowing lights, smoke, and paint splatters. Here you learn how to melt an object into the surrounding surface.

STEP 1   Select **File > New** to open the New document dialog box. From Preset choose Photo, from Size select Landscape, 5×7, and click OK. Set the foreground color to a neutral gray with the hex value of #d5d5d5 and fill the background layer with that gray by selecting **Edit > Fill** and choosing Foreground Color from the Use menu.

STEP 2   Find a stock image that you'd like to apply the melting effect to, such as a rubber ducky, a clock, a martini glass, or a pair of ice hockey skates and open it in your Photoshop workspace.

Press D to reset the colors, click the Add Layer Mask icon at the bottom of the Layers panel, and press X to make black the foreground color. Using a hard-edged Paint Brush tool (B), paint away the background areas of your object, leaving only the object visible. Change the brush size and hardness as needed to make a clean mask edge around the object.

When you have finished, drag a copy of this layer (with its mask) into your blank 5×7 file, and then close the original object image file.

STEP 3   In your 5×7 document, drag the object layer's mask thumbnail into the Delete Layer icon at the bottom of the Layers panel. When the dialog box opens asking if you'd like to apply the mask before deleting, click Apply.

Duplicate (Ctrl+J/⌘+J) the object layer and select **Edit > Transform > Scale** to resize the image so that it is flattened vertically by about half the original image's height. Then move the flattened layer below the original layer in the Layers panel.

STEP 4   Now comes the fun part! Select the flattened object layer and press Shift+Ctrl+X/Shift+⌘+X to open the Liquify dialog box. Select the Forward Warp tool (W) with a 300 px brush size and smudge the pixels along the left and right edges towards the bottom outer edges, as if tracing the sides of a volcano. Repeat as needed to create a melting effect. If you need to undo, click the Reconstruct or Restore All buttons. Otherwise, click OK when you are satisfied with your melted object.

Now select the Eraser tool (E) and with a large, hard-edged brush, gently erase away the bottom of the original object layer so that it blends nicely with the melted object layer. Select both the original and melted layers in the Layers panel and press Ctrl+E/⌘+E to merge them. Figure 56-1 shows an example of a pair of hockey skates on a gray background before Step 3 (top) and after Step 4 (bottom).

STEP 5   Press Shift+Ctrl+X/Shift+⌘+X to open the Liquify dialog box again. This time smudge the two parts of the merged image together so the overlap looks seamless, and then click OK to exit the dialog box.

Press Ctrl+J/⌘+J to duplicate the layer, select **Edit > Transform > Flip Vertical** to flip the duplicate, move the duplicate layer below the original layer in the Layers panel, and position the upside down object at the bottom edge of the original object.

Figure 56-1

To make the upside down object look like the reflection of the melted object, press X to make white the foreground color. Then press G to select the Gradient tool, and on the Options bar, choose Foreground to Transparent from the Gradient menu and select Linear Gradient as the gradient type. Then drag a gradient from the bottom of the document to the lower third of the right-side-up object to cover up the bottom of the upside-down copy.

STEP 6   The melting object needs a surface to sit on, so find an image of pavement, water, or some other texture and paste it into your file. Adjust that layer's opacity to around 20%. Use the **Edit > Transform > Perspective** command to adjust the perspective of the surface layer so that it looks as if it is receding into the background. Then use a wide, soft-edged, white Brush tool (B) to paint a mist along the top half of the textured surface to give the illusion of the distance clouded in mist.

To add a bit more mist around the object, create a new layer above the top-most layer in the Layers panel, set the opacity to 60%, and use the same large white brush to dab a few misty clouds around and atop the melted object.

STEP 7   The rest of the layout is entirely up to you. Have fun and play around with it. Figure 56-2 shows an example of how you might finish your layout. Here are some suggestions:

- Add a lens flare to a shiny part of the melted object.
- Duplicate the melting object two or three times, scale down the copies, reduce their opacity, and place them to the left and right of the main melted image.
- Add some penguins, polar bears, or ice cubes to the scene.
- Duplicate the melted object layer and apply the Plastic Wrap filter with the Hard Light blending mode.
- Scratch up the supporting surface layer (as if it were ice, plastic, or glass) with a 1 px white brush.
- Create a new layer below the melted object and add a shadow beneath it with a reduced opacity.
- Add a Hue/Saturation Adjustment layer to colorize the scene.
- Add some text or other ad copy.
- Use the Dodge and Burn tools to give more accurate shadowing under your melted object.

Figure 56-2

TECHNIQUE

57

CREATING RETRO HALFTONES

WHEN YOU SAY the word halftone, most designers immediately think of Roy Lichtenstein's paintings, and then promptly abandon the idea of using halftones in their work, for fear of making work that screams Pop Art. But there is a way to use halftones in Photoshop that is fresh and modern.

STEP 1   Open a fun image in Photoshop, like a picture of a skateboarder, and duplicate the image (select **Image > Duplicate**), leaving the original file open in the workspace.

Within the duplicate file, click the Hue/Saturation icon on the Adjustments panel and set the saturation to –100 to remove all the color. To isolate the subject from the background, double-click the locked background layer to turn it into a regular layer. Then use the Selection tools, Pen tool, or Quick Mask mode to select the entire background behind the subject, press Shift+Ctrl+I/Shift+⌘+I to inverse the selection, and add a Layer Mask by clicking the Add Layer Mask icon at the bottom of the Layers panel. Name this layer *subject* and drag a copy of this layer (with its mask) into your original document, but leave the duplicate file open.

STEP 2   Return to the duplicate file to convert the image into halftone dots. Click the Threshold icon in the Adjustments panel, and adjust the levels slider up or down to a point where the image has good contrast and definition. Then press Shift+Ctrl+E/Shift+⌘+E to merge all visible layers.

Next, select **Image > Mode > Grayscale**. When the dialog box opens asking if you'd like to discard color information, click the Discard button. Select **Filter > Blur > Gaussian Blur** to add a 3 px radius blur and click OK. Now select **Image > Mode > Bitmap**. When prompted to discard other channels, click OK, and when the Bitmap dialog box opens, enter an output value to match the input value. Select Halftone Screen as the method from the Use menu, and then click OK. In the Halftone Screen dialog box that opens, set the frequency to 30 (this determines the size of the halftone dots; the larger the number, the smaller the dots), set the angle to 45°, set the shape to Round, and then click OK. Select **Image > Mode > Grayscale**, and then select **Image > Mode > RGB Color**. Name this layer *halftone*. Figure 57-1 shows an original image next to its halftone version.

STEP 3   Drag a copy of the halftone layer into the original file above your masked layer in the Layers panel. To change the overall color scheme, click the Add New Fill or Adjustment Layer icon at the bottom of the Layers panel and choose Solid Color. When the Color Picker dialog box opens, set the hex value field to #4b0808 (maroon) and click OK, and then press Alt+Ctrl+G/Option+⌘+G to clip this color layer to your halftone layer. Don't be alarmed that you only see a solid color in your document window; there's more to come. Ctrl+click/ ⌘+click the thumbnail of your masked layer, press Shift+Ctrl+I/Shift+⌘+I to inverse the selection, click the Add New Fill or Adjustment Layer icon again and this time select #227178 (teal) in the Color Picker dialog box. You should now have a two-tone silhouette image like the one shown in Figure 57-2.

236

Figure 57-1

Figure 57-2

STEP 4   With teal layer selected, Ctrl+click/⌘+click the thumbnail of the subject layer, add a new Solid Color Adjustment layer filled with #f5efe1 (cream), and hide all three color fill layers by clicking the eye icon to the left of those layers. Then select the halftone layer and use the magic wand to select all the black areas. Toggle the visibility back on for the three hidden layers, select the cream Color Fill layer's thumbnail mask, press the X key to ensure that white is the top color in the toolbar, and then press the Delete/Backspace key and deselect. Your image should now be showing with three colors, as illustrated in Figure 57-3.

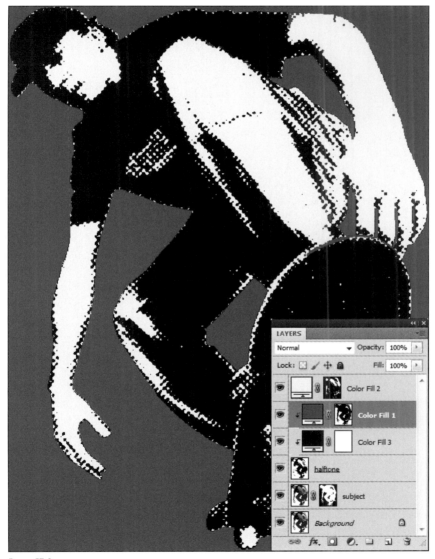

Figure 57-3

238

STEP 5   Now you'll add color to other areas of the subject. Use your Lasso tool (L) to draw a selection around a specific area of your subject. For example, in this picture you might create a selection of the skateboard. Fill the selection with a Solid Color Adjustment layer and drag this layer below the beige Color fill layer.

Repeat making selections and filling them with different color layers on new layers. For added effect, play around with the blending modes and opacity of the color fill layers. Figure 57-4 shows an example of a completed retro halftone image.

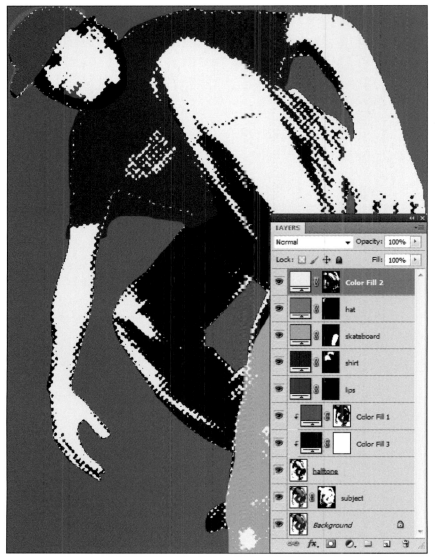

Figure 57-4

TECHNIQUE

58

MAKING TRIPPY RAINBOW PSYCHEDELIC SWIRLS

ALTON KELLEY AND Rick Griffin, two of the founding fathers of the Psychedelic Art movement, introduced trippy rainbow swirls in their psychedelic posters and album covers of the 1960s. Today you can create your own rainbow swirls in Photoshop without ever having to pick up a paintbrush or pen.

STEP 1 Select **File > New** to open the New document dialog box and select the size and resolution you will need for your final image. Or, for this example, choose U.S. Paper from the Preset menu and click OK.

STEP 2 Press G to select the Gradient tool On the Options bar, click the arrow to the right of the gradient thumbnail to open the Gradient Picker, and choose the Spectrum (rainbow) gradient, and then further down the Options bar, select Difference from the Mode menu. Take the Gradient tool and click and drag it across the document diagonally several times, from one corner to the other, back and forth, to create billowy rainbows with the look of folded silky fabric, like the example shown in Figure 58-1.

Figure 58-1

STEP 3 Press Shift+Ctrl+X/Shift+⌘+X to open the Liquify Filter dialog box, and use the Turn Clockwise tool (C) with a large 500 px brush to twist the rainbow stripes into fragmented bursts. This may cause some of the edges of your rainbow to bend inward, thus creating areas of transparency. Use the Forward Warp tool (W) to smudge away any blank areas back out past the edges. When you're satisfied, click OK to exit the dialog box. Your rainbow layer should now look something like the example in Figure 58-2.

STEP 4 Use your new trippy psychedelic swirls layer as a background element in a poster, as a fill pattern for letters and shapes, or as a clipping path pattern fill for an object within a layout, as illustrated in Figure 58-3.

241

Figure 58-2

Figure 58-3

TECHNIQUE

59

CONVERGING HORIZON LINES

CONVERGING HORIZON LINES are a series of alternating colored lines that converge at a center point and then increase in size as they radiate outward. This bursting effect is especially effective for giving your work a sense of power, movement, and excitement. Surprisingly, creating converging horizon lines is quite simple; here you learn two methods.

STEP 1   Select **File > New** to open the New document dialog box. Under Preset, choose Web, set the width to 500, the height to 400, and click OK.

STEP 2   For the first method, fill the background with the color or radial gradient of your choice, and then select the Custom Shape tool (U) from the toolbar. On the Options bar, click the Custom Shape menu to view the pop-up panel, click the arrow in the upper-right corner of the panel, and select the Symbols category to load those shapes into your menu. When the dialog box opens asking if you want to replace or append your current shapes, click Append, and then scroll down the menu and select the Registration Target 2 shape.

Shift+drag across your document to create a giant target shape with lines that extend all the way off the edges, and fill this shape with a hex value of #166c85. If desired, add a different shape on a separate layer to hide the center circle, as illustrated in Figure 59-1.

Figure 59-1

STEP 3   The second method, which uses a custom pattern, produces lines that fully converge at the center point. Open a new 30×30 px file and set the background to #f085c9. With your Rectangular Marquee tool (M), select a 10 px wide off-center vertical selection and fill it with color #ea1717. Press Ctrl+A/⌘+A to select all, select **Edit > Define Pattern**, and then close the pattern file.

STEP 4   Back in your other document, hide all the layers except the background, click the Add New Fill or Adjustment Layer at the bottom of the Layers panel, and select Pattern. When the pattern dialog box opens, you should immediately see your pattern fill the entire document window. To make the pattern lines converge, select **Filter > Distort > Polar Coordinates** and when prompted to rasterize the layer, click OK. In the dialog box that appears, choose Rectangular to Polar, and click OK. As you can see in Figure 59-2, the lines meet at a sharp point in the center of the file. Sweet!

Figure 59-2

CREATING A SCREEN PRINTING EFFECT

THERE IS NO denying the unusual appeal of a rough screen-printed image. This is due in large part to the printing process itself whereby a printing press forces ink through a woven mesh onto a supporting surface such as paper, cotton, or wood. Another reason for this old-school technique's appeal is the fact that it is used frequently on cool items of interest, such as posters, band flyers, and t-shirts.

STEP 1 Select **File > New** to open the New document dialog box. From Preset choose Photo, set the document size width to 9 inches, the height to 6 inches, and click OK.

STEP 2 Arrange one or two images in your file for a mock promotional postcard, and then merge all the layers with a white background layer. Then, to remove all the color, press Ctrl+Shift+U/⌘+Shift+U to desaturate the image completely.

STEP 3 Select **Image > Adjustment > Shadows/Highlights**. Set the shadow amount to 15%, the tonal width to 50%, and the radius to 30 px. Set the highlights amount to 20%, the tonal width to 50%, and the radius to 30 px. Click OK. Now select the Burn tool (O) and use it to burn in any shadow areas that could use a little more definition.

STEP 4 To make the image look like it's been photocopied from a newspaper, select **Filter > Noise > Add Noise,** and when the dialog box opens, set the amount to 15%, the distribution to Gaussian, leave Monochromatic checked, and click OK. Then apply a Gaussian Blur filter with a radius of 1.0 px.

Crank up the photocopier look even more by selecting **Filter > Sharpen > Smart Sharpen**. When the dialog box opens, set the amount to 300% and the radius to 30 px, then click OK. Repeat adding the Smart Sharpen filter, only this time set the amount to 100% and the radius to 50 px.

STEP 5 Copy the photo layer into a separate document and apply a halftone filter by selecting **Image > Mode > Grayscale**. Then select **Image > Mode > Bitmap**, match the output value to the input, select Halftone Screen from the Method menu, and click OK. When the Halftone Screen dialog box opens, set the frequency to 23, the angle to 45°, the shape to round, and click OK. Your image should now look somewhat like the example in Figure 60-1.

247

Figure 60-1

STEP 6   Select **Image > Mode > Grayscale** and then **Image > Mode > RGB Color**. Press Ctrl+J/⌘+J to duplicate the layer and then change the blending mode to Multiply. Select the original background layer, set the foreground color to #96dee, and fill the layer with that color.

Press Shift+Ctrl+N/Shift+⌘+N to add a new layer, change the foreground color to #d6e9a9, and use a hard-edged Brush tool (B) to paint a rough background area behind the main image in your layout, as shown in Figure 60-2.

Figure 60-2

STEP 7   The last step is to add some text to your layout. For instance, you might want to make a postcard advertising a B-movie night. Once you have the type laid out to your satisfaction, rasterize it by selecting **Layer > Rasterize > Type**, and then use the Eraser tool (E) with a distressed brush to erase away parts of the lettering.

Press D to reset the colors and press X to put white on top. Create another new layer, use the Lasso tool (L) to select an area around the most important part of the text, and fill the selection with white. Change the foreground color to #599193, add one more new layer, and paint a rough border around the outer edges of the layout. The completed screen printing effect is shown in Figure 60-3.

Figure 60-3

TWISTING THE KALEIDOSCOPE

A KALEIDOSCOPE IS a mirrored tube, often filled with tiny colored objects, that fragments and aligns a view of those objects at regular-angled intervals, thereby creating a wonderful multipart, mirrored image. In other words, the kaleidoscopic image is a symmetrical pattern created from duplicating a slice of an image at regular intervals. For example, a single image can be made up of six duplicate images when the mirror is angled at 60°. Likewise, a 90° angled mirror combines four images, and a 45° angled mirror combines eight images. Photoshop makes it easy to twist your own kaleidoscopic images from any sampled photo or illustration.

STEP 1   Start by opening an interesting photo into Photoshop. The best images for this technique include bright colors and strong lines. For example, you might want to use a photograph of some colorful foliage.

Grab the Rectangular Marquee tool (M) and Shift–drag to create a square selection around a segment of the image you find interesting, as illustrated in Figure 61-1. Press Ctrl+C/⌘+C to copy the square, press Ctrl+N/⌘+N to open the New document dialog box (the presets of which will automatically match the size and resolution of your selection), and then click the OK button. Press Ctrl+V/⌘+V to paste the selection into the new file.

Figure 61-1

STEP 2   Use the Polygonal Lasso tool (L) to select a triangle shape that cuts diagonally across the square, enclosing the part of the image you want to use for the kaleidoscope. Press Shift+Ctrl+I/Shift+⌘+I to inverse the selection, and then press Backspace/Delete to delete the remains. You should now have a single triangle shape on its own layer.

STEP 3   Select **Image > Canvas Size** and when the dialog box opens, set both the width and height fields to 200%, and make sure that the anchor is positioned in the top-right corner before clicking OK.

Duplicate the triangle layer by pressing Ctrl+J/⌘+J, flip the duplicate layer horizontally by selecting **Edit > Transform > Flip Horizontal**, and position the flipped triangle layer to the left of the first triangle so that both pieces form a downward-facing triangle, as shown in Figure 61-2.

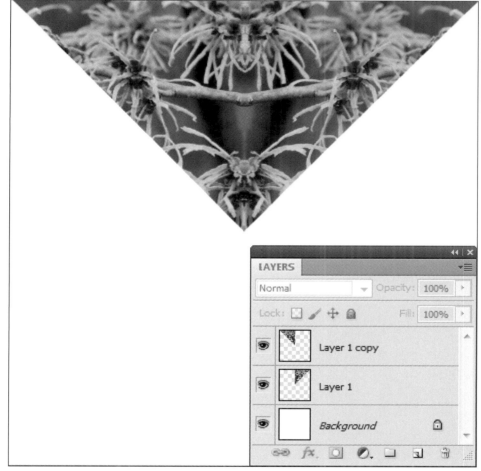

Figure 61-2

STEP 4   Merge the two triangle layers by selecting both and pressing Ctrl+E/⌘+E. Make a duplicate of this merged layer by pressing Ctrl+J/⌘+J, flip the duplicate vertically by selecting **Edit > Transform > Flip Vertical**, and position the new layer directly under the other so that the triangle points touch.

Now select both layers and make a merged duplicate of them by pressing Ctrl+Alt+E/
⌘+Option+E, and then rotate the duplicate 90° counter-clockwise by selecting **Edit >
Transform > Rotate 90 CW°**. If needed, use the arrow keys to nudge the up- and down-facing
arrow layers to form a seamless kaleidoscope image.

For an added twist, try adding smaller copies of the finished kaleidoscope to the center of the
original kaleidoscope image. Figure 61-3 shows an example of a kaleidoscope image (top) next
to a version with two smaller copied and rotated kaleidoscope images at its center (bottom).

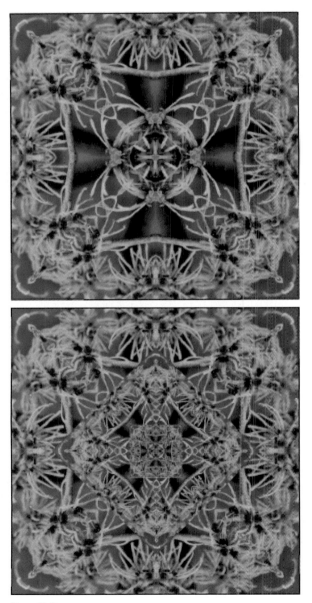

Figure 61-3

BUILDING A SURREAL LANDSCAPE

SURREAL LANDSCAPES ARE especially useful for imbuing a subject with a sense of wonder and amazement. Finding the photo that fits this prescription, however, can prove difficult unless you make it yourself in Photoshop. Grab two photos—one of a sky and one of a textured surface—and follow these steps to learn how to make your own surreal landscape.

STEP 1   Select **File** > **New** to open the New document dialog box. Under Preset choose Photo and from the Size menu select Portrait, 5×7, then click OK.

Now open up your sky and ground photos in separate document windows. When selecting (or shooting) the photos for your surreal landscape, use a sky shot with lots of clouds and a textured ground surface shot from a slight angle, as shown in Figure 62-1. Drag both images, one at a time, into your new blank document, and then label each layer appropriately (such as *ground* and *sky*), placing the sky above the ground in the Layers panel.

Figure 62-1

STEP 2   Add a layer mask to the ground layer by clicking the Add Layer Mask icon at the bottom of the Layers panel, select the mask and use a black Brush tool (B) to paint away, or hide, the parts in the image that aren't needed. Repeat this process for the sky layer. For best results, use a hard-edged brush to mask the ground and a large soft-edged brush to mask the sky. This will create a nice, clean edge like the example in Figure 62-2.

Figure 62-2

STEP 3   For a moodier vibe, click the Black & White icon on the Adjustments panel (either with or without a tint—your call) to convert the image to black and white. Next, click the Brightness/Contrast icon to increase the contrast to about 45.

Add a new layer at the top of the Layers panel and add a vignette by making an oval selection with the Elliptical Marquee tool and then inverting the selection by pressing Shift+Ctrl+I/ Shift+⌘+I. Next, click the Refine Edge button to add a 45-pixel feathered edge, click OK to exit the dialog box, and select **Edit > Fill** to fill the selection with black. Then change the layer's blending mode to Soft Light. The last step to complete your surreal landscape is to add some kind of object or subject to the center of your image, like the apple in Figure 62-3.

Figure 62-3

CREATING WATERCOLORFUL EXPRESSIONS

TECHNIQUE
63

THERE IS SOMETHING free about watercolor brush strokes. Maybe it is because watercolors seem more playful and expressive than oils or acrylics, or maybe watercolors seem more fresh and modern because you can often see the actual brush strokes through the medium. You can add watercolor expression to your layouts by downloading and installing custom brushes (or creating your own) and then using them in your work. To see how easy it is to express yourself with watercolors in Photoshop, follow the steps here to create a poster for train travel.

INTERNET HINT: Before you begin, download and install the free Photoshop watercolor brush set from Jay Hilgert at http://www.bittbox.com/freebies/free-hi-res-watercolor-photoshop-brushes and follow the onscreen instructions to install the brushes on your computer.

STEP 1   Select **File > New** to create a new file. Under Preset choose the U.S. Paper or International Paper option and click OK. In the center of your file, paste in an image of a train or other mode of transportation, as shown in Figure 63-1.

Figure 63-1

STEP 2   When adding colored brushstrokes to your file, you can either place each color on its own layer and adjust the blending modes for different blended effects, or simply paint all the colors on the same layer and leave the blending mode at Normal. Here are the suggested watercolor brushes and colors used to create the image in Figure 63-2:

- Paint the sky with blue #008dd0 using Sampled Brush 9 at 600 px.
- Paint the grass below the transportation image with light green #cbdc4c using Sampled Brush 9 at 620 px.
- Paint the grass below the light green with Sampled Brush 15 at 450 px using #46b973.
- Paint the grass at the bottom with Sampled Brush 12 at 860 px with #17a262.
- Paint the light white/blue wisps (like abstract clouds) with Sampled Brush 11 at 1750 px using #def24f.

Figure 63-2

STEP 3   Create a new blank layer above your color layer(s) and paint some more grass in the center of the file using #cadc4a with the brush of your choice, and change the blending mode to Linear Burn. This layer, as illustrated in Figure 62-3, really adds depth to the image.

Figure 63-3

STEP 4   To finish your poster layout, drop in some ad copy like the example in Figure 63-4.

Figure 63-4

TECHNIQUE

64

SIMULATING SPLATTERED PAINT EDGES

DESIGNERS ARE ALWAYS looking for new ways to spice up their images, doing anything from creating unusual text treatments to making wild custom special effects. Thanks to the advent of custom brushes, one of the new techniques you can add to your repertoire is the ability to make an object look as if its edges are splintering into splatters of paint. All you need to get started are a few sets of free splatter brushes and a picture of an object you'd like to splatter, such as a motorcycle or a bass guitar.

STEP 1   Download and install a free set of Photoshop splatter brushes from the Web, then select **File** > **New** to create a new file. Under Preset, choose photo, set the size to 5×5 inches, and click OK. In the center of your file, paste an image of the object (with the background cropped away) you'd like to apply the splatter effect to, as shown in Figure 64-1.

Figure 64-1

INTERNET HINT: Download a set of free splatter brushes from http://www. smashingmagazine.com/2008/10/22/splatter-and-watercolour-brushes-for-photoshop/.

To install the brushes, open the Brush panel (F5) and click the arrow in the upper-right corner, then click Load Brushes. From there, navigate to and select the downloaded brush .abr file to add it to your Brush libraries.

STEP 2   With your object layer selected, press Shift+Ctrl+N/Shift+⌘+N to create a new layer for your splatter marks and make sure your Color panel (F6) is showing. Click the foreground color swatch on the Color panel and sample a color from the edge of your object. Now press B to select the Brush tool, press F5 to expand the Brush panel, and select your first splatter brush. Use the settings within the Brush panel to control the size and rotation of the brush, and then apply the brush to the edge of your object. For best results, dab your brush along the object's edge rather than dragging it.

STEP 3   Repeat this process—sampling colors, choosing a brush, adjusting the brush features, and painting splatters—along the edge of your object as many times as necessary until you're happy with the results.

STEP 4   Duplicate the original object layer, hide the original layer, and using a hard-edged medium-sized Eraser tool (E), slowly erase away the edges of the object that you replaced with paint splatters.

For a touch of added realism, add a drop shadow beneath your subject. Figure 64-2 shows two different examples of this technique.

Figure 64-2

HINT: *To clean up the edges of your splatters (which can sometimes be a bit blurry and unrefined), use a sharpening filter on the splatter layer.*

V

SPECIAL

EFFECTS

TECHNIQUE

65

PASTING INSIDE SELECTIONS

HIDING UNDER PHOTOSHOP'S **Edit > Paste Special** menu are a two unique commands, Paste Into and Paste Outside. These commands let you paste a cut or copied selection inside or outside of a new selection within the same or another image. What makes these particular commands so distinctive is that fact that, upon pasting, the source selection goes onto its own new layer while the destination selection is turned into a layer mask, either hiding or revealing the pasted content. In effect, the pasted object appears more integrated with the underlying image than when performing a regular paste command, where the pasted object often looks pasted on top of everything else. This technique is especially useful with photo collages and commercial advertising.

STEP 1   Select **File** > **New** to open the New document dialog box. Under Preset, choose Photo; under Size select Landscape, 5×7, and click OK.

STEP 2   For this technique, you need two images, one as the *source* and one as the *destination*. For instance, you might want to start with a picture of a billboard (destination) and another picture to place on that billboard (source), like the images shown in Figure 65-1.

Figure 65-1

Open both images and copy them onto separate layers in your 5×7 file, and label the layers *source* and *destination*. If needed, resize the images to ensure that they will both have the same pixel dimension and resolution.

STEP 3   Select the source layer, press Ctrl−A/⌘−A to select all, press Ctrl+C/⌘+C to copy the source image onto the Clipboard, press Ctrl+D/⌘−D to deselect the selection, and then hide the visibility of the source layer in the Layers panel.

STEP 4   Select the destination layer and use your preferred selection tools to make a selection of the area you will paste the source image into. Click the Refine Edge button to add about 45 px of smoothing to the selection edges, and then click OK.

STEP 5   Select **Edit > Paste Special > Paste Into** to paste the source image into the destination selection. In the Layers panel, notice that the pasted image layer contains an unlinked mask, allowing you to freely move the pasted image behind the mask using the Move tool (V) when the image thumbnail is selected.

STEP 6   Scale the pasted source image by selecting its thumbnail in the Layers panel and pressing Ctrl+T/⌘+T to bring up the transformation bounding box. Adjust the size using the bounding box handles, and then press Enter/Return to accept the transformation.

To correct the perspective of the pasted image, select **Edit > Transform > Perspective** and adjust the bounding box handles as needed, then press Enter/Return to accept the transformation.

For a final touch of realism, click the Add Layer Style button at the bottom of the Layers panel and add the Inner Shadow style with both the distance and size set to 3 px, and then click OK. Figure 65-2 shows an example of the completed technique.

© Dmitriy Melnikov - Fotolia.com

Figure 65-2

271

WORKING WITH CUSTOM BRUSHES

FREE CUSTOM BRUSHES are available all over the Web and, as you've already seen in Techniques #63, "Creating Watercolorful Expressions," and #64, "Simulating Splattered Paint Edges," you can use these brushes to create all kinds of unusual and interesting effects. However, did you know that you can easily create your own brushes in any shape or size as well as control the brush behavior? The possibilities are truly endless.

With each custom brush you create, you'll follow the same workflow: first you create the brush artwork. Then you define the brush. After that, you select the brush and edit the brush behavior before using it in your file. Here you'll learn how to create three brush types; a simple shape, an abstract shape, and a photo brush.

STEP 1   Select **File > New** to open the New document dialog box. Under Preset choose Web, set the width to 500, the height to 500, and click OK.

STEP 2   For the simple brush shape, press Shift–Ctrl+N/Shift+⌘+N to add a new blank layer, press D to reset the toolbar colors to black and white, select the Elliptical Marquee tool (E), and Shift+drag a circle in the center of your file roughly 60 px in diameter. Next, select **Edit > Fill** and fill the selection with black, and then press Ctrl+D/⌘+D to deselect.

Select **Edit > Define Brush Preset** and name your new brush *dots*.

Hide the visibility of the layer with the single dot, press (B) to select the Brush tool, and then select your new brush from the Brush Preset Picker menu on the Options bar. Your new dots brush should be located at the bottom of the menu. With your dots brush selected, press F5 to open the Brush panel, click the Brush Tip Shape category at the top left, and adjust the size to 23 px and the spacing to 160%.

Now set the foreground color to #c81d1d, press Shift+Ctrl+N/Shift+⌘+N to create a new layer, and paint a row of dots across your file, as shown in Figure 66-1.

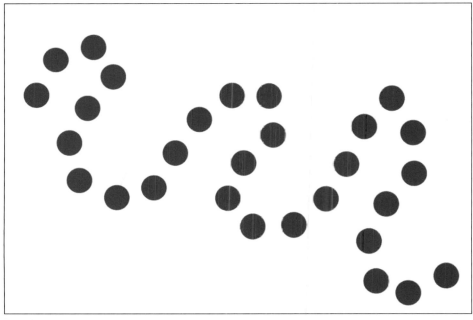

Figure 66-1

STEP 3 To make an abstract shape custom brush, hide the visibility of the red dots layer, and press Shift+Ctrl+N/Shift+⌘+N to add a new blank layer. Press D to reset the toolbar colors, select the Lasso tool (L) and draw a closed abstract blobby shape similar to the example shown in Figure 66-2. Then select **Edit > Stroke** and apply a 3 px black stroke to the selection. Select **Edit > Define Brush Preset** and name your new brush *blob*.

Hide the visibility of the blob shape layer and add a new blank layer above it. Press (B) to select the Brush tool and choose the new blob brush from the Bush Preset Picker menu on the Options bar. If desired, press F5 to open the Brush panel and modify any of the brush settings, such as the angle, smoothing, or size.

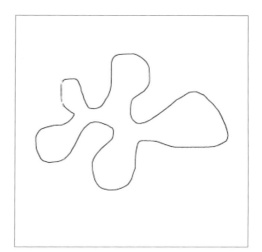

Figure 66-2

With your new blank layer selected, paint a swirl of blob shapes across your file as shown in Figure 66-3.

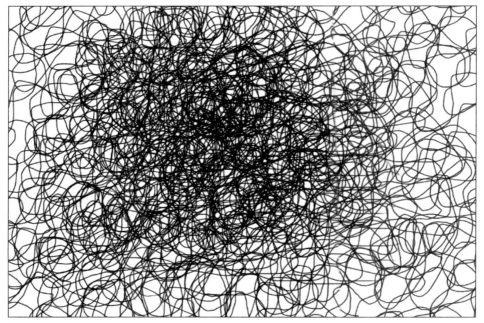

Figure 66-3

STEP 4   For the third custom brush—a photo brush—open a photo in a separate window that contains an image with a strong recognizable outline, such as a coffee cup, an airplane, or a bicycle. Using your preferred selection tools, make a selection of the object, add a new layer, hide the original photo layer, and fill your selection with solid black. With just the filled object layer showing, select **Edit > Define Brush Preset**.

To use your photo brush, open up another photo of a scene that you can use your photo brush shape in, such as a landscape or indoor scene. Select the new object brush from the Bush Preset Picker menu and click once to apply the brush to your photo. Figure 66-4 shows an example of a custom airplane photo brush.

Figure 66-4

SEWING STITCHES

LIKE BELL BOTTOM pants and platform shoes, stitching was a very popular fashion trend in the 1970s, and ever since then it has made several fashion comebacks roughly every 15 years or so. Be at the forefront of the next stitching wave by creating your own custom brush that looks like machine-sewed cross-stitching.

STEP 1   Select **File > New** to open the New document dialog box. Under Preset choose Web, set the width to 640, the height to 480, and click OK.

> *INTERNET HINT: You will need some sample fabric swatches to "sew" on. Before you begin, go to http://webtreats.mysitemyway.com/8-tileable-fabric-texture-patterns/ and download the free fabric pack to your desktop. You'll learn how to install them in a later step.*

STEP 2   With the Background layer selected, click the Add New Fill or Adjustment Layer icon at the bottom of the Layers panel, choose Solid Color from the menu, and set the color to #ddd4c9.

Click the Add Layer Style icon and apply a Pattern Overlay. When the Layer Style dialog box opens, click the Pattern menu button to open the Pattern Picker, then click the little circle arrow on the top-right of the picker window, select Load Patterns from the menu, navigate to your desktop and select the downloaded webtreats-fabric-patterns.pat file from Step 1. This will load the patterns into the bottom of your Pattern Picker window. Select the second blue jeans swatch called fabric_4-512px.jpg, set the Pattern Overlay Opacity to 34%, and click OK.

STEP 3   Select the Custom Shape tool (U), click on the Shape menu on the Options bar, then click the little circle arrow at the top-right of the picker window and select Shapes from the pop-up menu. After adding these shapes to the menu, find and select the heart shape, and Shift+drag a large heart across the center of your file.

With the shape layer selected, click the Add Layer Style icon at the bottom of the Layers panel and apply a Pattern Overlay. This time, select the Gray Jersey Knit texture called fabric_3-512px.jpg and click OK.

STEP 4   Open a new 160×160 px Web file, select a hard-edged 18 px brush, and draw an X shape in the center of the file, similar to the one shown in Figure 67-1. Then select **Edit > Define Brush Preset** and name your new brush *cross-stitch*. Now close the X file and return to your open document with the heart shape.

Figure 67-1

STEP 5   With your heart shape layer selected, press Shift+Ctrl+N/Shift+⌘+N to add a new blank layer and name it *cross-stitching*. Select the Brush tool (B), select your new cross-stitch brush from the Brush Picker menu on the Options bar, then press F5 to open the Brush panel so you can tweak the brush settings. Click the Brush Tip Shape category at the top-left and adjust the size to 12 px and the spacing to 110%. Then select Shape Dynamics category and set the Angle Jitter to 2% and the Angle Jitter Control menu to Direction. Press F5 again to hide the Brush panel.

277

STEP 6   To make the thread for your stitching, change the foreground color to #d8b13b, Ctrl+click/⌘+click the heart layer thumbnail mask to select the shape, switch over to the Paths panel, and click Make Work Path from Selection at the bottom of the Paths panel. Now click the Stroke Path with Brush icon at the bottom of the Paths panel to add the stitching around the heart. If your Stroke Path with Brush icon is grayed out, go back to the Layers panel to make sure the cross-stitching layer is selected, then try again. Your file should now look like the example in Figure 67-2.

Figure 67-2

STEP 7   With the cross-stitching layer selected, click the Add Layer Style icon at the bottom of the Layers panel and apply a Bevel and Emboss style. Set the Technique to Chisel Soft and the size to 0 px. Before closing the Layer Style dialog box, add the Drop Shadow style with the opacity set to 80%, the distance to 0%, and the size to 0 px, and then click OK.

STEP 8   Add a text layer with the word **LOVE** across the center of the heart in a simple sans-serif font, and Ctrl+click/⌘+click the text layer thumbnail mask to select the letter shapes. Press Shift+Ctrl+N/Shift+⌘+N to create a new layer, go to the Paths panel and click the Make Work Path icon at the bottom of the panel, then click the Stroke Path with Brush icon at the bottom of the Paths panel to add the stitching around the letters. Repeat the instructions in Step 7 on the *love-stitching* layer to add the same layer styles.

If you'd like to change the color of the thread on either of the stitching layers, select the layer, click the Lock Transparent Pixels icon at the top of the Layers panel, change the foreground color to the desired thread shade, and choose **Edit > Fill**. Figure 67-3 shows a finished version of the love heart stitching.

Figure 67-3

279

STENCILING EDGES

A *STENCIL* IS a template, made from some kind of sturdy material like cardboard or plastic, that a lets you paint or draw multiple, identical symbols, shapes, patterns, and text onto another surface. In the world of visual art, this technique is called *pochoir*, which is the French term for template. More recently, this technique has been co-opted by graffiti artists and graphic designers who use stencils with spray paint for a grungy, anarchistic effect.

STEP 1   Select **File > New** to open the New document dialog box. Under Preset choose Photo, select Portrait, 5×7 from the Size menu, and click OK.

STEP 2   In a separate window, open another file of an image you'd like to turn into a stencil, such as a chain link fence or a military tank. Make a selection of the main subject, copy it, and paste it onto a new layer. Then select **Image > Adjustment > Threshold** and adjust the image so that the white areas contain enough contrast to make out the subject in the image. Hide the original image layer, select **Edit > Copy Merged**, and then paste this black and white image into your original open file.

STEP 3   Choose **Select > Color Range** and use the eyedropper to sample the black within the new layer, and click OK to create a selection. Next, click the Add New Fill or Adjustment Layer button at the bottom of the Layers panel, choose Solid Color, and fill the selection with black.

Now Ctrl+click/⌘+click the thumbnail of this new layer to select the pixels, press Shift+Ctrl+N/Shift+⌘+N to add a new layer, select **Edit > Fill** to fill this selection with black, and drag this new layer below the Color Fill layer. Name this layer *airbrush*.

STEP 4   With the airbrush layer selected, apply a Gaussian Blur Filter with a Radius of 5 px, and then use a small splatter brush with the Airbrush Mode enabled in the Options bar to add a bit of paint here and there along the edges of the blurred layer. This will help to make it look as if paint seeped through the edges of the stencil. Figure 68-1 shows an example of a chain link fence before and after applying this airbrush/stencil effect.

INTERNET HINT: Download a set of free splatter brushes from http://www. smashingmagazine.com/2008/10/22/splatter-and-watercolour-brushes-for-photoshop/.

Figure 68-1

STEP 5   Open another interesting image of a person or object in a separate window and repeat Steps 2–4. This time, however, after you bring the layer into your main file and select the blacks with the Color Range command, create a new layer, lock down the transparent pixels of that layer, and apply a Linear Gradient to the selection using any two hues in the Foreground and Background color swatches, like the man silhouette in Figure 68-2.

STEP 6   Now it's time to play around and have fun. Add more layers of images with gradients, erase areas so white shows through, and adjust the perspective of images. Put a textured background behind all the layers, use some custom shape brushes, and add some paint splatters (see Technique #64, "Simulating Splattered Paint Edges") here and there for a rough and tough artsy look. Figure 68-3 shows an example of a finished stencil layout.

Figure 68-2

284

Figure 68-3

TECHNIQUE

69

MAKING SMOKE

WHILE SMOKING TOBACCO may be bad for your health, creating smoke in Photoshop is completely harmless. The easiest way to make smoke, of course, is to use a custom brush set made from actual photos of smoke. But that's sort of cheating, isn't it? There are, in fact, a few different ways to make realistic-looking smoke in Photoshop without the help of photographs, special plug-ins, or custom brushes. Here you find the best of several techniques rolled into one.

STEP 1   Select **File > New** to open the New document dialog box. Under Preset choose Photos, select Portrait, 5×7 from the Size menu, and click OK. Change the Foreground color to a dark hue such as a deep midnight blue #08152a, and then select **Edit > Fill** to fill the background layer with this foreground color.

STEP 2   Press Shift+Ctrl+N/ Shift+⌘+N to add a new layer, press the X key to flip the white background color to the foreground, and use the Pen tool (P) to draw some curvy, billowy shapes like the ones in Figure 69-1.

STEP 3   Select the Burn tool (O), set the tool's Range on the Options bar to Highlights, and then click once on the white area of your billowy shapes. This prompts Photoshop to ask if you'd like to rasterize the layer. Click OK, and then use the Burn tool to add shadow areas to the centers of each of the billowy shapes. Next select the Dodge tool (O), which is under the same menu as the Burn tool, and keeping the Range set to Highlights, add a little brightness to the outer edges of your shapes, as illustrated in Figure 69-2.

STEP 4   Select **Filter > Distort > Wave**, leave the settings at their default positions, and click OK. Then immediately select **Edit > Fade Wave**, set the opacity to 46%, and click OK. Repeat the Wave and Fade Wave commands once more to give the billows a more ethereal effect.

STEP 5   Duplicate your billowy shapes layer by pressing Ctrl+J/⌘+J and selecting **Filter > Liquify**. Use the tools in the Liquify dialog box to drag the edges of the billowy shapes upwards, like tendrils of smoke, and click OK.

286

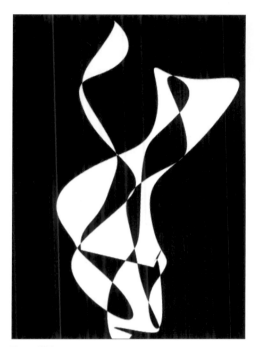

Figure 69-1

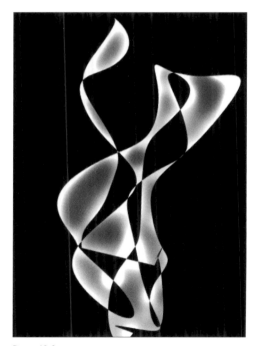

Figure 69-2

Select **Filter > Blur > Gaussian Blur**, set the radius to 12.0 px, click OK, and set the layer's blending mode to Multiply. To add a few subtle twists to the smoke-like shapes, select **Filter > Artistic > Plastic Wrap**, set the Highlight Strength to 15, the Detail to 10, the Smoothness to 7, and then click OK.

STEP 6   Merge all three of the layers by pressing Ctrl+E/⌘+E, then press Shift+Ctrl+N/ Shift+⌘+N to add a new layer on top. Use the Lasso tool (L) to make a blob-like selection around the smoke. Click the Refine Edge button on the Options bar, add a 40 px feather in the Refine Edge dialog box, and click OK. Then select **Filter > Render > Clouds**, change the layer's blending mode to Screen, the opacity to 17%, and click OK.

If your smoke contains any hard or uncon- vincing edges, soften them out using the Smudge tool. For a final touch of mood lighting, add another layer above the clouds, apply a Black to Transparent linear gradient to it with the blending mode set to Soft Light, and set the opacity to 74%. The finished effect should look similar to the example in Figure 69-3.

Figure 69-3

287

TECHNIQUE

70

CREATING WABI SABI STAINS

ALL DIGITAL DESIGNERS—regardless of whether they are creating projects for print, video, or the Web—should strive to avoid making work that looks too flat, spotless, and one-dimensional. This happens frequently to new designers who often stop before a project is truly complete. Besides adding elements that provide a degree of dimensionality such as drop shadows, one of the best ways to fight against computerized flatness is to introduce some kind of evidence of the imperfect human touch to your work, such as a hand-created watermark, coffee stain, tape mark, or tear. This idea is in perfect alignment with the Zen aesthetic of *Wabi Sabi*, which honors the imperfect.

STEP 1   Before you begin your design in Photoshop, get out a few pieces of blank copy paper and a cup of tea or coffee, and make your own set of stained papers that includes cup rings, splatters, splotches, and drips. For one of the sheets, dab liquid over the entire surface to give it a nice overall stain. Let all of your pages dry overnight and then scan them into Photoshop. Figure 70-1 shows an example of two custom stain pages: one with drips and cup rings and the other with an allover stain.

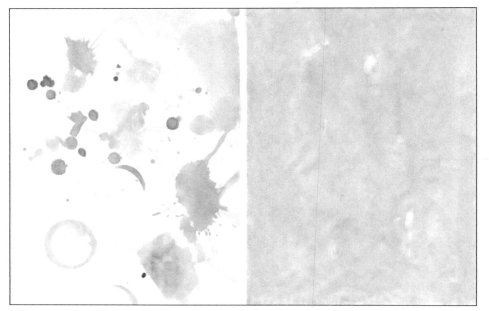

Figure 70-1

STEP 2   Press Ctrl+N/⌘+N to create a new business card file. Select Photo from the Preset menu, set the width and height to 3.5×2 inches, and then click OK.

STEP 3   Open a copy of your scanned file with the all-over stain and drag a copy of it into your document to use as the background. Next, open the scanned file with the cup ring stain, select the ring with the Rectangular Marquee tool (M), copy and paste it into your document above the all-over stain layer, and change the blending mode of the ring layer to Multiply.

STEP 4   To add some depth to the layout, use the Polygonal Lasso tool to make a diagonal selection from slightly above the bottom-left edge to slightly above the middle-right edge. Click the Add New Fill or Adjustment Layer button at the bottom of the Layers panel, select Solid Color, and fill the selection with #ccb98d. Set that layer's blending mode to Linear Burn and the opacity to 62%, select the Shape Layer Mask thumbnail, and use a soft-edged brush (B) to soften the top edge, as illustrated in Figure 70-2.

289

Figure 70-2

STEP 5   To complete the layout of this business card, go back to Technique #42, "Arching Text Around a Center Point," drag a copy of the logo you created there into this file, and position the logo in the upper-left corner. Next, add an image of a coffee cup and position it in the lower-right corner. In the upper-right corner, add the words **COFFEE CARD** and **www. planetmocha.com**, and in the lower-left corner, add the words "**Enjoy one FREE coffee drink when you buy ten**" and add 10 little shape boxes with a white fill and a black 2 px stroke. Finally, add some special touches of realism such as a few drips from one of your scans, a drop shadow behind the coffee cup, and some steam rising from the cup's rim. Figure 70-3 shows a finished Wabi Sabi stain layout.

Figure 70-3

TECHNIQUE

71

MASTERING INTARSIA POLYHEDRA

IF YOU'VE EVER had the chance to see in person any of Fra Giovanni's wonderful trompe l'oeil Florentine Renaissance "Intarsia Polyhedra" (mosaics made from inlaid wood) from the early 1500s, you know how magnificent and awe-inspiring this type of craftsmanship can be. Every element in these masterful constructions are created from intricately cut pieces of different colored wood, such as walnut, beech, rosewood, oak, and fruitwoods. Over the years, artisans have continued to create inlays with not only wood, but also other materials such as ivory, shells, mother-of-pearl, colored stones, marble, and metals. Thanks to Photoshop, you too can become a neo-Florentine artisan.

STEP 1   Select **File > New** to open the New document dialog box. From Preset choose Photo, set the width and height to 5 inches, and click OK.

You will need four texture samples of colored wood or other materials to build your inlay: one to be the background support surface and three for the inlay materials.

> *INTERNET HINT: You can find a host of wonderful free textures at http://www. smashingmagazine.com/texture-gallery-wood-bark/.*

Open the texture files you want to use and place a copy of each one onto its own layer in your 5×5 file. Label each layer according to the order in which you will be using it. For instance, if using three woods and one metal, you might label the surface layer Wood 1 and the other layers Wood 2, Wood 3, and Metal 1.

STEP 2   Press D to reset the colors and make sure that the Foreground color is set to black. Select the Custom Shape tool (U) and on the Options bar, click the Custom Shape menu to view the pop-up panel, click the arrow in the upper-right corner of the panel, and select the Symbols category to load those shapes into your menu. When the dialog box opens asking if you want to replace or append your current shapes, click Append, and then scroll down the menu and select the 10 Point Star Frame. Shift+drag a large star shape onto the center of your file. Then add a smaller version of the same shape in the center of the first, as illustrated in Figure 71-1.

STEP 3   Select both shape layers and select **Layer > Rasterize > Layers**. Next, Ctrl+click/⌘+click the thumbnail of the smaller shape, select the Metal 1 layer, and click the Add Layer Mask icon at the bottom of the Layers panel.

Select the small shape layer again and use the Magic Wand tool (W) to select the inside of the shape. Then select the Wood 3 layer and click the Add Layer Mask icon at the bottom of the Layers panel.

Now select the large shape layer, use the Magic Wand tool to select the inside of that shape, and add a layer mask to the Wood 2 layer. Select the large shape layer again, Ctrl+click/⌘+click the layer's thumbnail to select it, press X to make sure black is the foreground color, select the mask of the Wood 3 layer and press Backspace/Delete, and then deselect by pressing Ctrl+D/⌘+D.

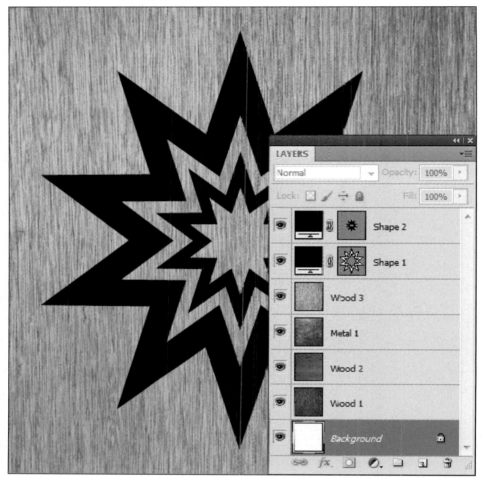

Figure 71-1

STEP 4   Use the Elliptical Marquee tool (M) to create a circle-shaped selection around the center of the largest star so that the edges of the circle extend past the star's inner points. Ctrl+Alt+click/⌘+Option+click the Wood 2 layer mask and press the Backspace/Delete key.

Use the Elliptical Marquee tool (M) again to create a larger circle-shaped selection so that outer edge extends roughly one-third inside of the outer points of the larger star. Ctrl+Alt+click/⌘+Option+click the Wood 2 layer mask, select the Metal 1 layer's mask, and press the Backspace/Delete key.

Now hide the visibility of the two shape layers to reveal your handiwork. Figure 71-2 shows the completed wood inlay effect.

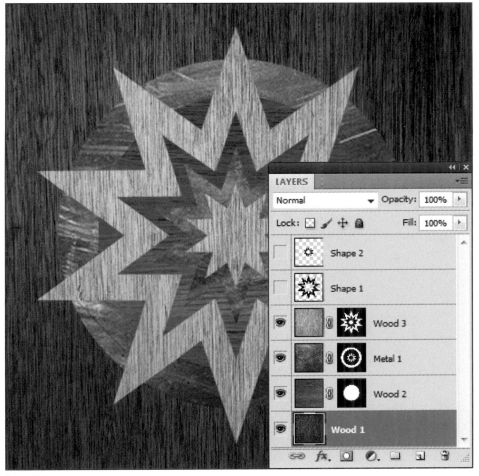

Figure 71-2

CREATING MODERN PAPER DOLLS

ALTHOUGH TOYS MADE from paper have been around for hundreds of years, the first manufactured paper doll was the Little Fanny produced in London back in 1810. Inspired by fashion, cultures of the world, celebrities, holidays, and patriotism, each paper doll often came with several sets of interchangeable clothing including dresses, gowns, coats, hats, shoes, gloves, costumes, and assorted accessories such as glasses, umbrellas, and handbags. Bring back a sense of nostalgia in your designs by creating your very own modern paper doll set.

STEP 1   Press Ctrl+N/⌘+N to open the New Document dialog box. From Preset choose U.S. Paper or International Paper, flip the dimensions so your file has a landscape orientation, and click OK.

STEP 2   Start by finding a good photo of a person in a stance that will be easy for you to interchange the clothing on top of. For instance, what often works best are poses where the person is standing with legs apart and arms either at the sides or in some kind of gesture, like the model shown in Figure 72-1.

Figure 72-1

STEP 3   Next, you'll need three sets of clothing for the figure to "wear." When looking for source photos, try to find garments and accessories photographed from the same angle as your model so that you can easily lay the clothing on top of the figure. Paste a copy of each garment into your open file on separate layers and then delete any unnecessary elements from the garment layers, such as limbs, hair, and background.

STEP 4 Use the Warp command (**Edit > Transform > Warp**) to adjust each garment and accessory to fit the pose of your model. When the Warp grid appears, drag the garment into the shape you need it to be, and then press Enter/Return to accept the transformation. Figure 72-2 shows an example of a source image, the same image cropped to show just the garment, and the garment after being warped.

Figure 72-2

STEP 5 Arrange each garment and accessory in a row to the left and to the right of the original model image. Press D and then press X to reset the colors and make white the foreground color, then select the background layer.

To create the tabs that will allow you to fit the cutout garments onto the model figure, select the Rectangle Shape tool (U) and drag out a small rectangle shape. Click the Add Layer Style button at the bottom of the Layers panel, choose Stroke, and apply a 1 px Black Outside Stroke to the rectangle, and then click OK. Press Ctrl+T/⌘+T to Free Transform the rectangle so that it peeks just behind the edge of the first garment.

Repeat this process until you have added tabs to the tops and sides of each garment and accessory. Figure 72-3 shows a completed Modern Paper Doll set.

Figure 72-3

TECHNIQUE

73

BUILDING A DOT RADIAL BACKGROUND

WITH HALFTONE IMAGES, the shape of the halftone dots are typically determined by the saturation levels within the image. Widely different saturation levels can produce results in a non-uniform dot pattern that is especially noticeable when you're trying to create a radial dot background behind the main subject in your layout. There is a way, however, to create a dot radial background using dots in a uniform circular pattern that diminishes in size.

STEP 1   Select **File > New** to open the New document dialog box. From Preset choose Web, set the width and height to 500 px, and click OK.

STEP 2   Use the Elliptical tool (U) to Shift+drag a large circle in the center of your file. Select the Horizontal Type tool (T) and set the font to Arial Rounded MT Bold, 200 pt (or any other font with round periods). Hover your cursor above the top edge of the shape and when the dotted lines around the cursor turn into a straight line (as if the cursor is surfing along the path), click once and type in enough periods to go around the entire circle, as illustrated in Figure 73-1.

> HINT: If needed, adjust the tracking on the Character panel to ensure that the spacing between each dot is even, paying particular attention to the first and last dot along the circular path.

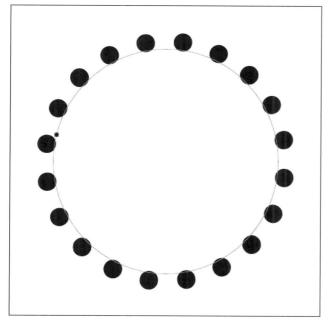

Figure 73-1

STEP 3   Right+click/Ctrl+click the text layer on the Layers panel to access the Context menu and select Convert to Shape. Press Ctrl+J/⌘+J to duplicate the layer, and then press Ctrl+T/⌘+T to scale the layer to be slightly smaller than the first. For best results, be sure to hold the Shift+Alt keys to constrain the shape proportions while scaling. Rotate the layer a tiny bit so that the smaller dots fit between the larger dots, and then press Enter/Return to accept the transformation.

Repeat this process of duplicating, scaling, and rotating, until you have seven layers of dots, like the example in Figure 73-2.

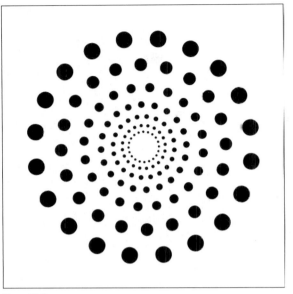

Figure 73-2

STEP 4   The last step is to change the Fill color of each of the shape layers to match the rest of your layout. Click the Lock Transparent Pixel icon at the top of the layers panel for each layer before adjusting the foreground color and choosing the **Edit > Fill** command.

Feel free to vary the number of layers, size of the dots, and distance between each ring. Figure 73-3 shows an example of how you might use your radial dots in an advertising layout.

Figure 73-3

FAKING WATER DRIPS

IN MANY PHOTOGRAPHS of food and drink, the more luscious, moist, and fresh the food appears, the more appetizing and appealing the results. That's why food stylists often use spray bottles full of diluted glycerin on their food shots for that fresh out-of-the-garden, just-washed-and-prepared look. If you can't afford a food stylist, however, you can fake those water droplets in Photoshop.

STEP 1 Select **File>New** to open the New document dialog box. From Preset choose Web, set the width to 500, the height to 500, and then click OK.

STEP 2 Lay out a scene for your food product using as many layers as you need, and blur the background layer to keep the focus on the product. Figure 74-1 shows an example of a simple layout with a table, milk bottle, and blurred cloud background.

Figure 74-1

STEP 3 Select the top layer in your Layers panel and press Ctrl+Shift+N/⌘+Shift+N to add a new layer. Then select the Brush tool (B), choose a small hard-edged brush around 10 px in diameter, and adjust the brush settings in the Brush Panel so that the Shape Dynamics, Scattering, Texture, Dual Brush, and Smoothing options are selected and configured as follows:

303

- Shape Dynamics: Set all the options to 0% and off, except for the Size Jitter Control menu, which should be set to pen pressure.

- Scattering: Increase the Scatter to 700%, put a check in the Both Axes checkbox, and set the count jitter to 95%.

- Texture: Set the scale to 100% and the mode to Linear Burn. Select a texture that looks water-like, such as the Clouds texture from the Patterns pattern library. Then put a check in the Texture Each Tip checkbox and set the depth to 75%.

- Dual Brush: Set the size to 100 px.

Take your brush and paint a few scattered dots down or across the side of your food object, as shown in Figure 74-2, and name this layer *water drops*.

Figure 74-2

STEP 4   Change the blending mode of the water drops layer to Lighten, then click the Add Layer Style button at the bottom of the Layers panel, and choose Bevel and Emboss. Change the size to 8 px and change the Shadow Mode color from black to a sampled color from the object beneath the dots (which should now look somewhat like water droplets), and then click OK.

STEP 5   Increase your brush size to 16 px and, on the same layer, add a few larger droplets toward the base of your object and then decrease your brush size to 4 px and add a few smaller droplets near the top of your object. For the most realistic effect, feel free to add or remove droplets as needed. Figure 74-3 shows an example of the effect in a completed layout.

Figure 74-3

MAKING A NA'VI AVATAR

WHETHER YOU'VE GONE to see the movie or not, you've no doubt been exposed to images of the Na'vi people—with their pointy ears, blue striped skin, large yellow-green eyes, and glowing freckles—from James Cameron's *Avatar* movie. With some patience and generous help from the Liquify panel, you too can make your own Na'vi avatar.

STEP 1   To begin, open a well-exposed photo of a person you'd like to turn into a Na'vi. Select the entire background behind the person using your favorite selection tool(s), click the Add New Fill or Adjustment Layer icon at the bottom of the Layers panel, select Solid Color, and set the fill color to black.

STEP 2   Use any of the selection tools to select the person's face and any other parts of the skin that are showing and click the Hue/Saturation icon on the Adjustments panel. Set the hue to -167, the saturation to +12, and the lightness to -15 to turn the skin blue. You may need to adjust these values depending on the color values of your starting image.

STEP 3   Select the thumbnail mask of the Hue/Saturation layer and use a small, black, hard-edged brush to paint away (hide) the blue hue over the eyes and mouth. Figure 75-1 shows an example of a person before and after adding the blue skin.

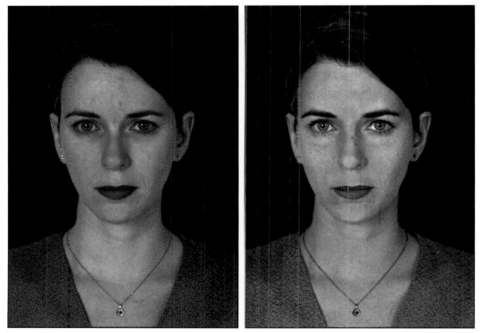

Figure 75-1

STEP 4   Again using your preferred selection tool(s), select the right ear, copy it, and paste it onto a new layer. Then select both ears and cover them up with a Solid Color Adjustment Layer filed with black. Move the copied ear layer to the top of the Layers panel, use the Warp command (**Edit > Transform > Warp**) to stretch and contort it into a pointy ear, and position the ear parallel to the eye on the same side of the face.

Press Ctrl+J/⌘+J to duplicate the ear layer, flip it horizontally by selecting **Edit > Transform > Flip Horizontal**, and position this new ear across from the first ear. Now select both ear layers and merge them by pressing Ctrl+E/⌘+E, and apply the same Hue/Saturation values to the merged ears layer from Step 1.

HINT: If you'd like to keep each ear unique for a more realistic end result, repeat the first part of this step for the left ear rather than duplicating the right ear layer.

Select the thumbnail mask from the ears Hue/Saturation layer, make sure that white is set as the foreground color, and press B to select the Brush tool. On the Options bar, set the size of the brush to 35 px with a soft edge and the opacity set to 50%, and gently paint away the insides of the ear, as illustrated in Figure 75-2.

Figure 75-2

STEP 5 Open the Liquify panel (**Filter > Liquify**) and use the Bloat tool (B) with a 200 px wide brush to widen the nose. Start at the tip of the nose and click a few times until you reach the bridge. For the eyes, place the crosshair in the center of each iris, and then click and hold for the count of three. Use the Reconstruct or Restore All buttons as needed until you are satisfied with your distortions, and then press OK to accept your changes.

STEP 6   To smooth out the distortion of the widened nose, use the Dodge and Burn tools to add shading along the left and right sides of the nose. Then to give the nose a pinkish tip, use the Lasso tool to select the tip of the nose, click the Refine Edge button to add a 5 px feather, create a new layer by clicking the Create New Layer icon at the bottom of the Layers panel, and paint the selection using #875b7b with 30% opacity. Choose **Select > Deselect** and adjust the blending mode to Multiply.

STEP 7   Use the Elliptical Marquee tool (O) to select the iris in one of the eyes. Then click the Add New Fill or Adjustment Layer icon at the bottom of the Layers panel, select Solid Color, set the fill color to #d2a220, and set the blending mode to Soft Light.

To ensure that the pupils stay rich and black, select the thumbnail eye mask of the color fill adjustment layer, make a circular selection around the pupil, and delete it from the mask. Repeat this process with the other eye, so the eyes look similar to the example in Figure 75-3.

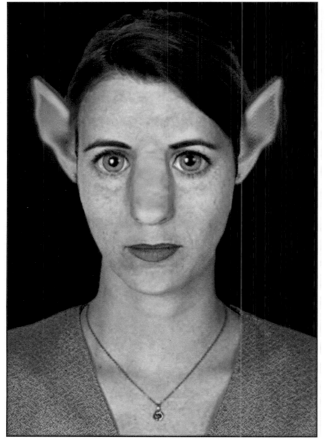

Figure 75-3

STEP 8   To finish the transformation, add some details such as outlining the lips, adding a crease at the tip of the nose, striping the skin, adding freckles, and cleaning up the hairline.

If you can find a zebra print pattern, clip it to your original Hue/Saturation mask layer, change the opacity to 10%, and use the Eraser tool (E) to erase any areas that fall below the bridge of the nose and below the eyes. Otherwise, create some stripe shapes using the Pen tool (P) and set the opacity of each shape layer to 10%.

For the glowing freckles on the skin, add a new layer, give it an Outer Glow layer style with the color set to #b2d5f1, and then add the dots using a 9 px soft-edged brush with white paint and the brush opacity set to 45%.

Lastly, select all the layers, merge them onto a new layer (Alt+Ctrl+E/Option+⌘+E), and use the Smudge tool to clean up the hairline. Figure 75-4 shows a completed Na'vi transformation next to the original source file.

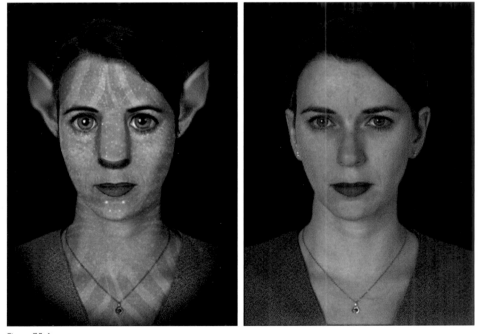

Figure 75-4

> HINT: If you'd like to further enhance your Na'vi character, consider arching the nose slightly into the eyebrows and adding some fake hair extensions on either side of the face in front of the ears.

TECHNIQUE

76 TRACING PHOTOS

WELL-CRAFTED TRACED photos take time and care, along with knowing the right settings and tools to use in Photoshop. To create a good tracing, you can use one (or both) of two methods described here. The first involves painting with various sized brushes, whereas the second involves creating and stroking paths and is far more time consuming but may produce better results. Experiment with both techniques and use the one that gives you the results you are seeking.

STEP 1   Bring the photo you want to trace into the Photoshop workspace and click the Create a New Layer icon at the bottom of the Layers panel twice. Label the first layer *paths* and the second layer *paint.*

STEP 2   Press F5 to open the Brush panel (or select **Window > Brush**) and select the Brush Tip Shape category at the top of the panel. Set the size of the brush to 5 px, the angle to -150, the roundness to 30%, the hardness to 100%, and the spacing to 3%. Next, click the Shape Dynamics category, set the control to Fade with a value of 230, and set the minimum diameter to 45%. Press F5 again to hide the panel.

STEP 3   For the painting method, select the paint layer, zoom into one of the features of your image (such as the ear), and begin painting the outlines of the shape. Vary the brush size as needed using the bracket keys ([and]) to emphasize the shape in a more natural way.

Repeat this process for the other features of your subject: outline of the face, edges of clothing, and other details. You may either add each brush stroke to the same layer, or create new layers for each feature. Figure 76-1 shows an example of a painted outline next to the original file.

Figure 76-1

STEP 4   For the path and stroke method, hide the visibility of the paint layer(s), select the paths layer, select the Pen tool (P), and on the Options bar, select Paths. Zoom into the first facial feature, trace the path of that shape, Right+click/⌘+click on the path, and select Stroke Path from the Context menu. When the Stroke Path dialog box appears, select Simulate Pressure, check to make sure that brush is showing in the Tools menu, and click OK.

To darken any particular line, stroke the path two or three more times after the first stroke. In addition to making open shapes with the Pen tool, create closed shapes with other tools where needed and select Fill Path instead of Stroke Path from the Context menu. To delete the path after stroking or filling, choose Delete Path from the Context menu.

Repeat this process for each feature of your subject; adjust the outline of the face, the edges of clothing, and any other details within the image of importance. Figure 76-2 shows an example of a stroked path traced outline next to the original file.

Figure 76-2

313

MOCKING TILT-SHIFT SCALE MODELS

A TILT-SHIFT effect refers to the shallow depth of field that happens when a photographer shoots a subject from a high vantage point while shifting the angles between the two image planes of a large-format camera. Technically speaking, according to the Scheimpflug principle (named after the Austrian who devised it to take better aerial photographs), when the camera's lens and image planes are parallel but the plane of focus (PoF) is not, the image will only be in focus where the image plane intersects with the PoF. In other words, when the camera is set up in just the right way, the photographer can make the resulting image look like a miniature-scale model. With Photoshop, you can get a tilt-shift effect in your photographs without having to buy a large format camera or even a Photoshop plug-in.

STEP 1   Open the photograph you want to miniaturize in Photoshop. To get the best results from this technique, use a photo with a subject captured from a high angle, as with an image taken from a hilltop, airplane, bridge, or the window of a high-rise, like the image in Figure 77-1.

Figure 77-1

STEP 2   Duplicate the background layer and name it *tilt-shift*. Press Q to enter Quick Mask mode, D to reset the colors, X to put white on top, and G to select the Gradient tool, making sure to choose the Foreground to Background and Reflected Gradient settings from the Options bar. Drag a gradient from the center of the file upwards about half the way to the top and release. The starting point of your line will set the area of focus while the end of the line sets the spot where the blur completes its transition from focus to out-of-focus. After releasing your mouse, you will see a red gradient mask across the screen where you just drew your line, as illustrated in Figure 77-2.

Figure 77-2

STEP 3   Press Q to exit Quick Mask mode, and select **Filter > Blur > Lens Blur** to open the Lens Blur dialog box. Select Heptagon (7) from the Shape menu, set the radius to 44, set the blade curvature to 16, and then click OK.

If you don't quite like the way the focus is situated, undo through the History panel, return to the previous step, and try drawing the line in a different position. It may take a few tries to get the effect you have in mind, so be patient until you get it right.

STEP 4   Most real miniature-scale models are indoors under tungsten or fluorescent lighting. To mimic that effect, click the Hue/Saturation icon on the Adjustments panel and pump up the Saturation to around +32. Then, click the Photo Filter icon on the Adjustments panel, change the color to #ecb200, and set the density to 45%. Now click the Brightness/Contrast icon and set the contrast to 35.

STEP 5   Two additional modifications you may want to make are to add a little bit of a blur and a vignette along the left and right edges of the in-focus area. Select the Blur tool, choose a 1000 px soft-edged brush, set the strength to 100% on the Options bar, and gently apply the Blur brush to the outer edges of the focus area. Next select the Burn tool (O), choose a 1400 px soft-edged brush, set the range to Midtones, and gently brush along the outer four corners of the image. Figure 77-3 shows a finished example of this technique.

Figure 77-3

MIMICKING CROSS PROCESSING (XPRO)

CROSS-PROCESSING (XPRO) is a term used to describe when one type of color film is deliberately processed as if it were another. Most often this technique is used to process color positive slide film (which is normally processed in E-6 chemicals) as if it were standard color negative film using C-41 chemicals. Unlike color negative film, which has an orange base to help correct the film's ability to record shades of green and blue, color positive slide film has a colorless base. Therefore, by processing slide film as if it were negative film, you end up with negatives on a colorless base. When printed, these negatives produce color photographs with rich, high-contrast, often unpredictably surreal color saturation with deep blues in the shadow areas, magentas in the midtones, and a yellowish-green cast in the highlights. Digital photographers can easily simulate this effect in Photoshop using a handful of adjustment layers.

STEP 1   Open the photograph you want to cross-process, press Ctrl+J/⌘+J to duplicate the background layer, and use the Elliptical Marquee to select most of the image as one giant oval. Press Shift+Ctrl+I/Shift+⌘+I to inverse the selection, click the Refine Edge button on the Options bar, set the feather to 80 px, and click OK.

Click the Levels Adjustment icon in the Adjustments panel and move the midtones marker a little bit toward the right to darken edges like a vignette. Now Ctrl+click/⌘+click the thumbnail mask of the Levels Adjustment layer to reselect the oval shape, select the duplicate image layer, and select **Filter > Blur > Lens Blur**. When the dialog box opens, set the shape to Square (4), the radius to 35, the blade curvature to 10, and click OK to apply a slight blur to the selected area.

STEP 2   With the now-blurred duplicate image layer still selected, click the Curves icon on the Adjustments panel to adjust each of the channels under the Curve (RGB) as follows:

- Red Channel: Adjust the white and black points inwards along the top and bottom edges just a bit to add red.
- Green Channel: Add two center points and position them in a slight S curve, placing the right point near the highest peak on the right and the left point near the lowest peak on the left.
- Blue Channel: Repeat the midpoint placement like you did for the green channel.

Depending on the quality of the original exposure, you may need to adjust each channel to get the desired Xpro look.

STEP 3   Select the duplicate image layer again, click the Brightness/Contrast icon on the Adjustments panel, and bump up the contrast to 30. Then, to warm up the whole image, click the Photo Filter icon on the Adjustments panel, set the color to #ecc800, and set the density to 57%. The result should look something like the examples in Figure 78-1 and Figure 78-2, where the originals are on top and the Xpro versions are on bottom.

Figure 78-1

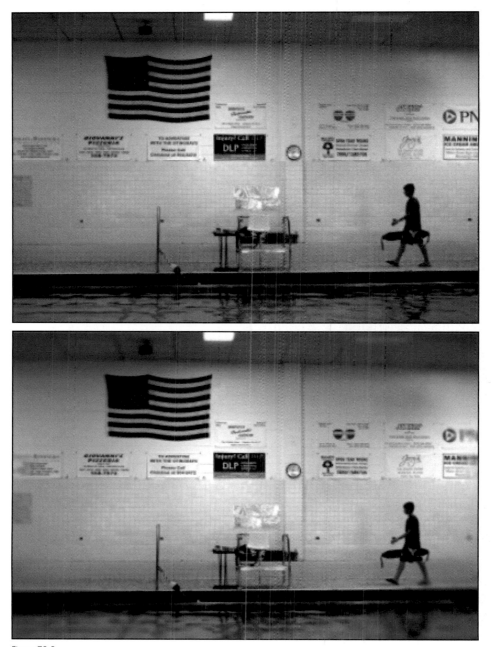

Figure 78-2

CREATING FIRE WITH THE SMUDGE TOOL

YES, THE DIGITAL fire effect has been around since the late 1980s, but unless you've ever had the need to use fire in a print, Web, or video layout, you may have no idea how to create this effect yourself. There are, of course, several methods for simulating fire, but by far the best technique involves the use of the incomparable Smudge tool.

STEP 1   Select **File > New** to open the New document dialog box. From Preset choose Web, set the width and height to 500 px, and then click OK.

Fire looks best against a dark background, so set the foreground color to #040b10, select the background layer, select **Edit > Fill**, and when the dialog box opens, select Foreground Color from the Use menu, and then click OK.

STEP 2   Next, you need something to add the fire effect to, such as a picture of your best friend, your ex, a motorcycle, or a guitar. Open the image (which should be at least 200–300 dpi) in a separate window, select the object (or subject) without any background, copy it, and paste it into your open file. You may then close the image source file.

STEP 3   Back in your open file, select the background layer and press Shift+Ctrl+N/ Shift+⌘+N to add a new layer. Then press G to select the Gradient tool and select a black and white foreground to background, radial gradient from the Options bar. Drag a small radial gradient behind the subject, and then set the opacity to 25%, as illustrated in Figure 79-1.

Figure 79-1

STEP 4   Select your subject layer, add a new layer above it (Shift+Ctrl+N/Shift+⌘+N), and then use the Lasso tool (L) to create a selection around the part of the object/subject you want to add flames to. Click the Refine Edge button on the Options bar, add a 20 px feather, and click OK. Press D, then X, then Shift+F5 (or select **Edit > Fill**) to fill the selection with white. Deselect the area by pressing Ctrl+D/⌘+D and name this layer *flames*.

> HINT: *Within the Refine Edge dialog box, you can change how the selection displays by choosing an option from the View menu. For example, you might prefer to view your selection on white (W), as an overlay (V), or with marching ants (M).*

STEP 5   Select the Smudge tool with an 80 px soft-edged brush, and drag the outer edges of the fuzzy white layer upwards, like little licks of flame. Now select **Filter > Distort > Wave** and set the number of generators to 4, the Type to Sine, the wavelength min and max to 10 and 130, the amplitude min and max to 5 and 30, and click OK. Immediately select **Edit > Fade Wave**, shift the opacity to 60%, and click OK. Figure 79-2 shows the example image before and after using the Smudge tool and Wave filter.

STEP 6   Ctrl+click/⌘+click the thumbnail of the flames layer and click the Hue/Saturation icon on the Adjustments panel. Click the Colorize option and set the hue to 36, the saturation to 100, and the lightness to +10. Now use a large soft-edged eraser (E) to erase away some of the flames layer for a more natural flames look. Continue by selecting the Hue/Saturation thumbnail mask and use a black, 80 px soft-edge brush (B) to erase away additional parts of the flame. Figure 79-3 shows the finished hot flame effect.

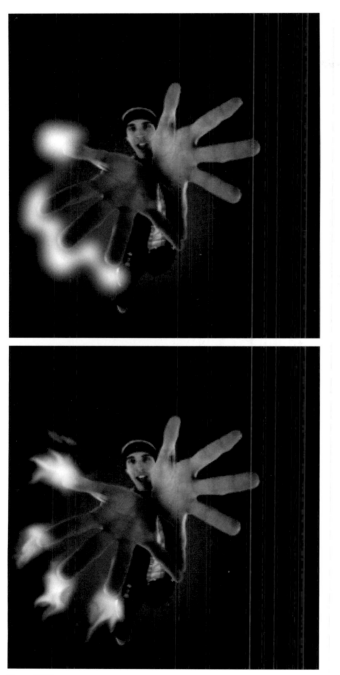

Figure 79-2

Figure 79-3

VI
IMAGE
DISTRESSING

80
TECHNIQUE

SIMULATING SEPIA-TONED IMAGES

IN A TRADITIONAL darkroom, photographers will often use toners on black and white photographs to help make the silver within the emulsion more stable. Some toners, like selenium, are used to aid in the preservation of the image, whereas other chemicals both improve the archival qualities and alter the overall tone or color cast of an image. Sepia toning, which was quite popular in the late 19th/early 20th century, gives black and white images a rich, warm tone that converts the blacks to browns and the whites to a light cream. Today, sepia-toned images conjure feelings of nostalgia for an old-fashioned, somber, bygone era, and with Photoshop you can give your digital photos that same Victorian era toned look without venturing into the darkroom.

STEP 1   Open your original color or black and white photo in Photoshop and make four copies of your original image layer.

There are actually several ways to apply a sepia tone to a digital image in Photoshop, so try each method to determine which one works best for your particular image.

To help keep track of each method, you should label the duplicate layers *Styles*, *Filters*, *Adjustments*, and *Duotone*, as illustrated in Figure 80-1.

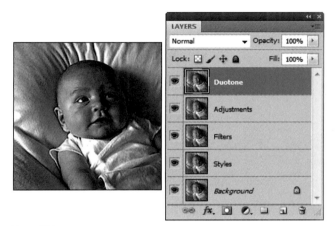

Figure 80-1

STEP 2   **Styles method:** Select the Styles layer and hide the visibility of all the other layers in the Layers panel. Open the Styles panel by selecting **Window > Styles**. Click on the Sepia Tone style icon.

That's it. The style is like an action that adds a Color Overlay layer style with the blending mode set to Color, the color set to #e1d3b3, and the opacity at 100%. Although this sepia has a bit of a green cast to it, the effect is actually quite good.

STEP 3   **Filters method:** Select and show the Filters layer and hide the visibility of all the other layers in the Layers panel. Click the Black & White icon on the Adjustments panel and click the Auto button to have Photoshop automatically adjust the color sliders for your image. If needed, adjust the sliders to add or subtract contrast from your image.

Next, click the Return to Adjustment List icon (arrow) at the bottom of the panel and click the Photo Filter icon. Choose Sepia from the Filter menu and adjust the density to about 85%. The last step is to add a Color Fill adjustment layer (**Layer > New Fill Layer > Solid Color**) filled with #250b00 and the blending mode set to Screen.

STEP 4   **Adjustments method:** Select and show the Adjustments layer and hide the visibility of all the other layers in the Layers panel. Duplicate the Adjustments layer, click the Hue/Saturation icon on the Adjustments panel, and set the saturation to 0%.

Reselect the duplicate layer and select **Filter > Blur > Gaussian Blur**. You don't need to add that much blur to soften the image, so set the radius to 1.0 px and click OK.

Next, click the Add Layer Style icon at the bottom of the Layers panel and select Color Overlay. Set the blending mode to Soft Light, the color to #7d6719, the opacity to 100%, and click OK. Finally, set the blurred duplicate layer's blending mode to Soft Light and reduce the opacity to 50%.

STEP 5   **Duotones method:** This method is actually best done in its own document window, so select the Duotones layer, making sure this layer is visible rather than hidden. Press Ctrl+A/⌘+A to Select All, press Ctrl+C/⌘+C to copy, press Ctrl+N/⌘+N to open the New document dialog box where you'll click OK, and press Ctrl+V/⌘+V to paste the image into the new file.

Select **Image > Mode > Grayscale**, and then select **Image > Mode > Duotone** to convert your image into a two-color grayscale image. When the Duotone Options dialog box opens, select Duotone from the Type menu, click on the square next to Ink 1, set the color to #ffc659, and name this ink *Sepia*. Then click on the Ink 2 square, select black, name the ink *Black*, and click OK. Finally, select **Image > Mode > RGB Color** to convert the file back into an RGB image.

Figure 80-2 shows the results of all four methods with the Styles on the top left, the Filters on the top right, the Adjustments on the bottom left, and the Duotone on the bottom right. Although none of these techniques exactly matches the true color of a sepia toned print, the Filters method definitely comes closest.

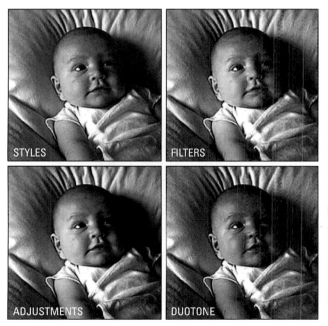

Figure 80-2

SIMULATING A VAN DYKE BROWN PRINT

A VAN DYKE Brown print is one of the early types of contact printing techniques that involve the use of UV light and large format negatives. Although typically printed on watercolor paper coated with a Van Dyke Brown solution, you can also use this technique on other treated surfaces such as wood, metal, or glass. After exposure, the resulting photographic image appears in tones of deep, rich, chocolaty brown instead of black. In fact, it was the rich tones that gave this technique its name, as the browns produced by this process are similar to the brown oil colors used by the Flemish painter Van Dyck. In addition to the unique tones, it is common to show the edges of the chemical coating surrounding the negative as part of the final image.

STEP 1   Open the image you want to convert into Van Dyke print in Photoshop. Nostalgic images tend to work best with this technique, but your image can truly be of anything you like, such as a portrait, landscape, singular object, or animal like the ostrich shown in Figure 81-1.

Figure 81-1

STEP 2   To give your document a watercolor paper texture, click the Add New Fill or Adjustment Layer icon at the bottom of the Layers panel and choose Color Fill from the menu. When the Color Picker dialog box opens, select #f7f5f3 as the fill color and click OK. Now click the Add a Layer Style icon at the bottom of the panel, choose Pattern Overlay, and set the blending mode to Multiply. Then click the Pattern menu button to open the Pattern Picker, click the little circle arrow on the top-right of the picker window, and select Artists Surfaces. Click the Append button to add these patterns to the bottom of the Pattern Picker, scroll down and choose Watercolor, and then click OK to close the Layer Style dialog box.

STEP 3   For the painted emulsion (light sensitive brown coating), click the Create a New Layer icon at the bottom of the Layers pane, rename the layer *edges*, and set the foreground color to #23100e. Press B to select the Brush tool, choose a nice wide watercolor brush from the Brush Picker menu (see Technique #63, "Creating Watercolorful Expressions," for details about downloading and using watercolor brushes), and paint across the center of the window, as illustrated in Figure 81-2.

STEP 4   Adding the Van Dyke Brown tone to your image comes next. Select your original background layer, press Ctrl+J/⌘+J to duplicate it, and move the duplicate layer above the edges layer. Click the Add a Layer Style icon at the bottom of the panel, choose Color Overlay, change the blending mode to Color, change the color to #422b28, and then click OK.

Figure 81-2

STEP 5   With your duplicate image layer still selected, press Ctrl+T/⌘+T to scale the image down to fit inside the painted area of the edges layer. Rename this layer *Van Dyke*.

STEP 6   The edges of your Van Dyke layer are too hard and even, so you need to roughen them up a bit. Ctrl+click/⌘+click the layer's thumbnail to make a selection around the image, and then choose **Select > Modify > Contract**. When the dialog box opens, set the Contract By amount to 50 px and click OK.

Without deselecting, press Q to enter Quick Mask mode and select **Filter > Brush Strokes > Splatter**. In the dialog box, set the Spray Radius to 12, the Smoothness to 13, and click OK. Press Q to exit Quick Mask mode, select Shift+Ctrl+I/Shift+⌘+I to inverse the selection, and then press Backspace/Delete to delete. Still without deselecting, select **Filter > Blur > Gaussian Blur**, set the radius to 15 px, and click OK. Now you can press Ctrl+D/⌘+D to deselect. Figure 81-3 shows the finished effect.

Figure 81-3

CREATING CYANOTYPES (BLUEPRINTS)

SIMILAR TO A Van Dyke Brown print (see Technique #81, "Simulating a Van Dyke Brown Print"), a cyanotype is an early photographic printing technique introduced by Sir John Hershel in 1842 and made popular shortly thereafter by the first female photographer, Anna Atkins. The process uses a special chemical emulsion of iron compounds and a UV light source to produce photographic images and photograms with deep cyan blue tones instead of black or brown. Also referred to as blueprints, artists often intentionally show their cyanotypes with the blue emulsion surrounding the negative as part of the final image.

STEP 1   Open the image you want to make into a cyanotype. The best images for this type of process are photos of easily recognizable objects or subjects, such as portraits of people or animals, close-ups of singular objects, or artsy formalist shots like the canoes in Figure 82-1.

STEP 2   Click the Add New Fill or Adjustment Layer icon at the bottom of the Layers panel and choose Solid Color from the menu When the Color Picker dialog box opens, select #f6f5ed as the fill color and click OK.

STEP 3   For the blue emulsion layer, click the Create a New Layer icon at the bottom of the Layers panel, rename the layer *edges*, and set the foreground color to #1e2b51. Press B to select the Brush tool, choose a nice wide watercolor brush from the Brush Picker menu (see Technique #63, "Creating Watercolorful Expressions"), and paint a rough-edged rectangle shape across the center of the window as illustrated in Figure 82-2.

STEP 4   Select your original background layer, press Ctrl+J/⌘+J to duplicate it, and move the duplicate layer above the *edges* layer. Click the Add a Layer Style icon at the bottom of the panel, choose Color Overlay, change the blending mode to Color, change the color to #72b3d9, set the opacity to 100%, and then click OK.

STEP 5   With your duplicate image layer still selected, press Ctrl+T/⌘+T to call up the Transform bounding box around the image so you can scale it down to fit inside the blue rectangle. Rename this layer *Cyanotype*.

STEP 6   Ctrl+click/⌘+click the Cyanotype layer's thumbnail to make a selection around the image, and then choose **Select > Modify > Contract**. When the dialog box opens, set the Contract By amount to 50 px and click OK.

Figure 82-1

337

Figure 82-2

Without deselecting, press Q to enter Quick Mask mode and select **Filter > Brush Strokes > Splatter**. In the dialog box, set the Spray Radius to 12, the Smoothness to 13, and click OK. Press Q to exit Quick Mask mode, and to inverse the selection, press Shift+Ctrl+I/Shift+⌘+I, and then press Backspace/Delete to delete. With the selection still active, select **Filter > Blur > Gaussian Blur**, set the radius to 15 px, and click OK. Then press Ctrl+D/⌘+D to deselect.

STEP 7   To give your image a watercolor paper look, click the Add New Fill or Adjustment Layer icon at the bottom of the Layers panel and choose Solid Color from the menu. When the Color Picker dialog box opens, select #ffffff as the fill color and click OK.

Now click the Add a Layer Style icon at the bottom of the panel, choose Pattern Overlay, set the blending mode to Soft Light, and set the opacity to 100%. For the texture, click the Pattern menu button to open the Pattern Picker, click the little circle arrow on the top-right of the picker window, and select Artists Surfaces. Click the Append button to add these patterns to the bottom of the Pattern Picker, and then scroll down and choose Coarse Weave. Adjust the scale to 350%, and then click OK to close the Layer Style dialog box.

Finally, adjust the layer's blending mode to Darken and the opacity to 7%. Figure 82-3 shows an example of a finished cyanotype effect.

Figure 82-3

TECHNIQUE 83

ADDING A VINTAGE VIGNETTE

VIGNETTE IS A term that refers to the darkened and slightly blurry areas around the outer edges of a photograph, which tends to make the viewers focus their attention on the center of the image. Vignettes can happen naturally under the right circumstances or can be created deliberately in camera through a combination of special lighting, camera settings, lenses, and lens filters. You can also add a vignette post-processing in the darkroom or in Photoshop.

STEP 1   Start by opening your image in Photoshop. There are two ways to create your vignette, depending on whether you want your final image to be in color or black and white. For best results, use one technique for color images and the other for black and white.

STEP 2   Color Vignette: To add a vignette to your color image, press Ctrl+J/⌘+J to make a duplicate of your background layer and name the duplicate layer *vignette*. Select the Brush tool (B), and with a soft-edged 1300 px brush, paint with black around the four corners and outer edges of the vignette layer, as illustrated in Figure 83-1.

Figure 83-1

Now change the layer's blending mode to Multiply or Soft Light to reveal the background image through the duplicate vignette layer. Figure 83-2 shows an example of the vignette effect (top) next to the original file (bottom).

> *HINT: Alternatively, you could paint with black on a blank layer and simply lower the opacity of that layer without changing the blending mode. Whichever method you choose to use, keep in mind that the final outcome is often dependent on the quality of the starting image.*

Figure 83-2

STEP 3   **Black and White Vignette:** To add a vignette to a black and white image, use the Elliptical Marquee tool (M) to drag a large oval selection in the center of the image. Click the Refine Edge button on the Options bar, set the feather to 250.0 px, and click OK. Then press Shift+Ctrl+I/Shift+⌘+I to inverse, select **Filter > Blur > Gaussian Blur**, set the radius to 2.5 px, and click OK.

> HINT: *If you're starting from a color image that you want to convert to black and white, click the Black & White icon on the Adjustments panel, and adjust the color sliders until you are satisfied with the contrast and tone of the image.*

Before deselecting the selection, click on the Black & White Adjustment layer in the Layers panel to select it, click the Levels icon on the Adjustments panel, and move the black point marker slightly to the right until the vignette appears across your image in the desired amount. When satisfied, press Ctrl+D/⌘+D to deselect. Figure 83-3 shows an example image before (top) and after (bottom) adding the vignette.

Figure 83-3

TECHNIQUE 84

MAKING DIGITAL IMAGES GRAINY

GRAIN IN PHOTOGRAPHY refers to the size of the tiny bits of silver within the film emulsion. With film, the higher the film speed (ISO), the larger the grain on the negative. When the negative is printed, the grain appears as scattered bits of dark and light across the image. Some photographers try to avoid having grain by shooting at lower film speeds with film larger than 35mm. Other photographers, however, covet this uniquely gritty feature of film and deliberately use high film speeds to increase the size of the grain. Although most digital cameras are now designed to take grainless photographs, there are two ways to produce grainy images digitally: you can shoot at a high ISO or you can add grain in Photoshop.

STEP 1   Like many things in Photoshop, there are several ways to achieve digital grain in your high-resolution images. Here you'll discover three techniques. To begin, open an image in Photoshop, create three duplicate layers of the image (Ctrl+J/⌘+J), and label them *A*, *B*, and *C*.

> *INTERNET HINT: For a clear and concise explanation about ISO and digital photography, see http://digital-photography-school.com/iso-settings.*

STEP 2   **Film grain method:** The first option uses the Artistic Film Grain Filter. Select the *A* layer and hide the visibility of all the other layers. Then select **Filter > Artistic > Film Grain**. When the dialog box opens, set the grain to 6, the highlight area to 2, the intensity to 3, and click OK. With this effect, you can control the amount the highlights get blown out, which can be a useful grungy effect in certain images. Figure 84-1 shows an example of how this filter looks (bottom) next to the original image (top).

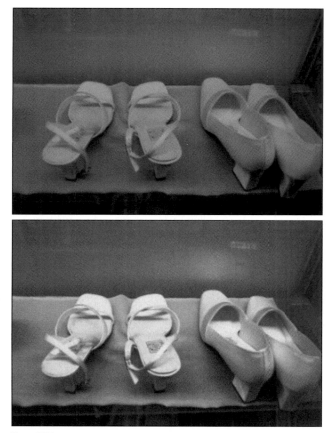

Figure 84-1

STEP 3   **Texture grain method:** For the second option, you'll use the Texture Grain filter. Select the B layer and hide the visibility of all the other layers. Then select **Filter > Texture > Grain**. When the dialog box opens, you'll see that there are several settings to choose from, depending on your intentions. For standard grain on a color image, for instance, select Regular or Soft from the Grain Type menu. Alternatively, to add lots of grain and turn a color image into black and white, select Stippled. Regardless of which style you choose, set the intensity to 40, the contrast to 60, and then adjust the sliders as needed to accommodate the exposure in your particular image. When satisfied, click OK. Look at Figure 84-2 to see examples of both the regular (top) and stippled (bottom) grain styles.

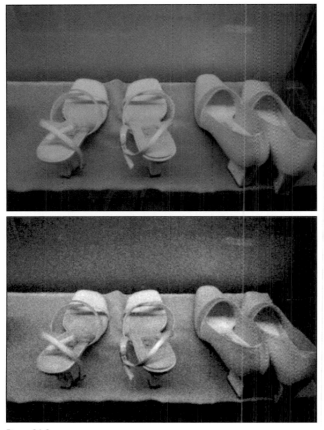

Figure 84-2

STEP 4 **Noise method:** The third technique involves working with the Noise filter, which you can apply directly to your image layer or, better yet, use on a layer filled with 50% gray.

Select the C layer and hide the visibility of all the other layers. Press Shift+Ctrl+N/Shift+⌘+N to create a new layer, select **Edit > Fill** to open the Fill dialog box, choose 50% Gray from the Use menu, and click OK. Change the gray layer's blending mode to Overlay, and then select **Filter > Noise > Add Noise**. Set the noise amount to 12%, the distribution to Uniform, leave the Monochromatic box checked, and click OK. Depending on the amount of grain you want to have visible, you may want to apply a slight Gaussian blur and/or reduce the opacity of the gray layer. Figure 84-3 shows an example of this noise effect.

> HINT: *When applying the Add Noise filter directly to an image layer, instead of a gray layer, choose Uniform either with or without the Monochromatic option for color images, or Gaussian for B&W images.*

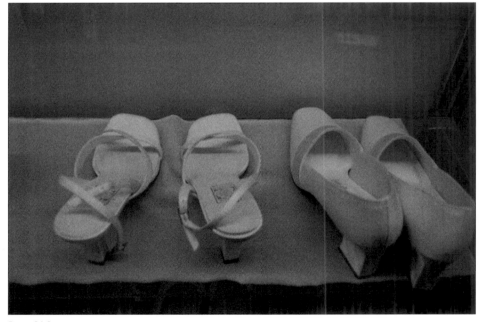

Figure 84-3

85

WEATHERING A PHOTO

THE DIGITAL PHOTO can be a double-edged sword. On the one hand, working digitally allows you to capture images with unsurpassed clarity and detail. On the other hand, digital files can at times be so crisp and clear that they appear lacking in the warmth, depth, and texture that you get when working with film and traditional printing processes. With Photoshop you can recapture some of that darkroom mystique by weathering your images. Besides making your digital files look as if they were printed using traditional materials, you can also make them look as if they've been left outside, stepped on a few times, beaten up, and otherwise mistreated.

STEP 1   Open your high-resolution image in Photoshop and start by adding some grain. Press Ctrl+J/⌘+J to duplicate your image and label the new layer *grain*. Select **Filter > Noise > Add Noise**, and when the dialog box opens, set the amount to 15%, the distribution to Gaussian, leave the Monochromatic box checked, and click OK.

STEP 2   With the grain layer selected, select **Filter > Blur > Gaussian Blur**, set the radius to 2.5 px, and click OK. Press Ctrl+J/⌘+J to duplicate this layer and name the duplicate *vignette*.

Select the Brush tool (**B**), and with a soft-edged 1000 px brush, paint with black around the four corners and outer edges of the vignette layer, and then change the blending mode to Overlay and set the opacity to 65%. Figure 85-1 shows an example of an image with just the added grain (top) and the same photo with both the grain and vignette layers visible (bottom).

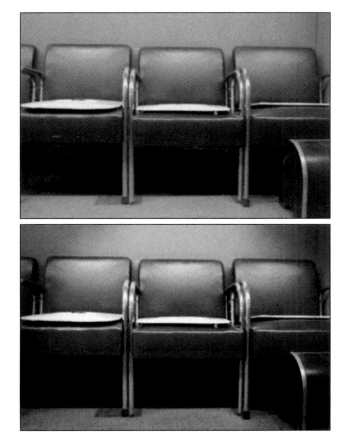

Figure 85-1

348

STEP 3   Select both the grain and vignette layers and merge them onto a new layer by holding down the Alt/Options key while selecting Merge Layers from the Layers panel menu.

Now hide the visibility of the original layers, and with the new merged layer selected, click the Add Layer Mask button at the bottom of the Layers panel, select the Brush tool (**B**) with a 1 px hard edge and paint two or three "tears" along the outer edges of the image using black paint. You can also paint in a few scratches on the layer here and there with both black and white, as illustrated in Figure 85-2.

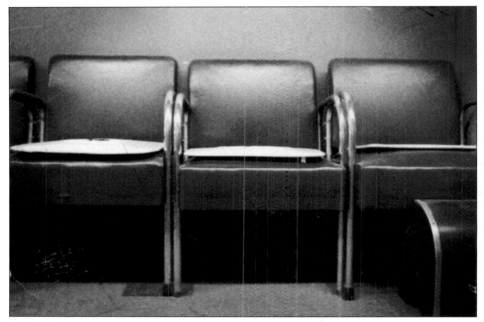

Figure 85-2

STEP 4   For a bit more texture and roughening of the image, paste a copy of an image of weathered cardboard or folded Kraft paper into the file on a new layer at the top of the Layers panel. Label this layer *texture*, change the blending mode to Pin Light, and set the opacity to 30%. To fade the brightness of the color, click the Hue/Saturation icon on the Adjustments panel and adjust the saturation down to -30.

STEP 5   The image looks good, but it could still use some visual damaging. Download and install (load) the free scratches brushes from http://www.photoshopbrushes.com/brushes/39. htm and use them in a random way on the texture layer to add a bit more of a grungified effect. Lastly, give the image a white 50 px white border (fill a selection with white) and use the scratches brushes to roughen the edges of this layer. Figure 85-3 shows an example of the artificially weathered image (top) together with the original (bottom).

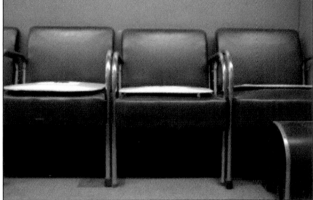

Figure 85-3

TECHNIQUE

86

SIMULATING A PLASTIC CAMERA

BACK IN THE 1970s, a couple of plastic toy cameras came on the market to make photography even more affordable to the masses. The images these cameras took were by no means high quality; however, there was definitely something uniquely appealing about them. The most notable brand was the Diana camera, but sadly as it grew in popularity it became harder and harder to find. After that, the jewel of the plastic camera world was the Holga from China, which offered appealing visually unpredictable results. Today, thanks to manufacturers in China and the folks at Lomography.com, toy cameras are readily available again in a variety of formats and styles for every budget. For the digital photographer who prefers to avoid the cost of film, processing, and darkroom duty, the dreamy toy camera effect (light leaks and all) can be yours in Photoshop.

STEP 1   Because many toy cameras use 120 film, the first thing you'll do after opening your image in Photoshop is to crop it into a square format. Select the Rectangular Marquee tool (M), hold down the Shift key, drag a square selection over the best part of your image, and then select **Image > Crop**.

STEP 2   Press Ctrl+J/⌘+J to duplicate your background layer and name the duplicate *blur*.

With the blur layer selected, use the Elliptical Marquee tool (M) to make a large selection over most of the image. Press Shift+Ctrl+I/Shift+⌘+I to inverse, click the Refine Edge button on the Options bar, set the Feature to 85 px, and click OK.

Now select **Filter > Blur > Lens Blur**, and, in the dialog box that opens, set the shape to Hexagon (6), the radius to 38, the blade curvature to 17, the rotation to 360, the brightness to 6, the threshold to 181, the noise to 1, and the distribution to Uniform. Make sure the Monochromatic option is checked, and then click OK.

Before deselecting, click the Levels icon on Adjustments panel and move the black slider to the right to darken the selection area. Then press Ctrl+D/⌘+D to deselect, select the mask thumbnail on the Levels Adjustment layer, and paint with an 800 px soft-edged black brush around the edges of the mask circle to make the circle less even. Figure 86-1 shows the original square image on left and a version with this blurred vignette on the right.

Figure 86-1

STEP 3 With the blur layer still selected, select **Filter > Noise > Add Noise**, and when the dialog box opens, set the amount to 3%, the distribution to Gaussian, and make sure the Monochromatic option is checked before clicking OK. Now choose **Filter > Distort > Diffuse Glow**. Set the graininess to 6, the glow amount to 10, and the clear amount to 15. Finally, wash out the colors a little bit by increasing the whites in a Levels Adjustment layer. Figure 86-2 shows the finished toy camera effect.

Figure 86-2

If desired, turn your image into black and white by clicking the Black & White icon on the Adjustments panel and adjusting the sliders to your liking, as illustrated in Figure 86-3.

Figure 86-3

TECHNIQUE 87

FAKING FADED FOLDED PAPER

IF YOU WANT your digital work to contain a sprinkle of realism, it's important to add a few subtle distress marks in your files. Besides being extremely cool looking, marks like creases, wrinkles, and tears in a piece of folded paper give digital art a little bit of the human touch, showing evidence of life and the process of decay. Unfortunately, filters, custom brushes, and layer styles alone can't recreate that type of authenticity, but with a little help from your printer, scanner, and Photoshop, you can make your own phony faded folded paper effect.

STEP 1 Open up a standard paper size document in Photoshop, press D to reset the colors, and select **Edit > Fill** to fill the entire background with black. Print this page and then immediately fold the printout in fourths, twist it, and unfold. Rub two areas of the black parts together to create some scratches and rub away some of the ink. Take an eraser or sandpaper to other parts of the page here and there until you can begin to see some of the ink starting to scratch off.

STEP 2 When you're happy with the distressing of your printed page, scan it and open the file in Photoshop. Click the Levels icon on the Adjustments panel, and in the Adjustments panel, brighten the whites by moving the midtone marker a little to the left. Figure 87-1 shows an example of a page that's gone through this process.

Figure 87-1

STEP 3 Now you need an image to use with the folded paper layer. Open your image file in a separate window, switch over to the open scanned file, press Ctrl+A/⌘+A to select all, and press Ctrl+C/⌘+C to copy it. Then close the scanned file.

Return to your open image file and go to the Channels panel. At the bottom of the panel, click the Add New Channel icon and press Ctrl+V/⌘+V to paste in your copied scan so it becomes a channel named Alpha 1. Ctrl+click/⌘+click the Alpha 1 thumbnail to load the creases as a selection, and press Ctrl+C/⌘+C to copy the selection.

STEP 4 Return to the Layers panel and press Shift+Ctrl+N/Shift+⌘+N to create a new layer, press D to reset the colors, and press Ctrl+Delete/⌘+Delete to fill the selection with white. Then press Ctrl+D/⌘+D to deselect the selection.

Depending on the desired outcome, you may want to adjust the opacity and/or change the blending mode to Overlay. Alternatively, if you're working from a color image and want it to be black and white, convert it by clicking the Black & White icon on the Adjustments panel.

Figure 87-2 shows the results of the phony paper effect (top) together with the original color image (bottom).

Figure 87-2

TEXTURIZING AN IMAGE

TECHNIQUE

88

IN ADDITION TO using Photoshop's presets and creating your own custom brushes, shapes, and patterns, you can also create custom textures from any material you can scan or photograph. Custom textures give your work unsurpassed depth, realism, and interest that would otherwise be missing. When searching for textures, look for images with lots of surface detail like rusted metal, cracked cement, peeling paint, crumbling walls, and other things in an obvious state of decay. Use your imagination and try taking detailed shots of anything that catches your eye, such as a light reflection on a wall, funky fabric, a spider's web, or a stack of yellowing old newspapers. The more unusual and unique your texture layers, the better the effect in your finished project.

STEP 1 For this technique, you'll need two texture files and one image file to use the textures in, such as a spider's web, a light reflection, and an indoor scene; something like the example images in Figure 88-1. Open all three high resolution files in the Photoshop workspace and make the indoor scene image the active document.

Figure 88-1

The following steps give you a general idea of how textures can improve your Photoshop layouts, whether they contain photos, flat areas of color, text, or a mixture of everything.

STEP 2 Press U to select the Rectangle tool to drag a 225 px tall rectangle shape across the lower third of the file and fill it with a neutral color such as #d4c7a8. Then select the Type tool (T) and add a few words in white text, in the font and size of your choice, across the rectangle, as illustrated in Figure 88-2.

Figure 88-2

STEP 3 Switch over to the first texture file, copy it (Ctrl+C/⌘+C) and paste it (Ctrl+V/⌘+V) into your indoor scene file. Label the pasted layer according to what is in the image (for example, *light reflections*), change the blending mode to Color Burn, and set the opacity to 50%.

Repeat the copy/paste process with the second texture file, only change the second layer's blending mode to Linear Light and the opacity to 50%. Now move the text layer to the top of the Layers panel.

If needed, adjust the blending mode and/or opacity of the texture layers to get the desired effect. Your image should now have some interesting texture and depth, as illustrated in Figure 88-3.

THE READING ROOM @ BALTHAZAR'S ALLEY   TUESDAYS @ 8PM

Figure 88-3

MAKING A PEELING PAINTED METAL EFFECT

HAVE YOU EVER noticed how painted metal signs look when they are faded and weathered? The outer edges of the paint or vinyl adhesive start to peel and crack, scratches and scrapes become more apparent, and in some instances, it can look as if entire bands of pigment have been stripped away from the original with sticky tape or a razor blade. To create a similar painted metal effect within the solid color filled shapes, text, and other flat areas in your own layouts, all you need is another image with lots of lines and angles and a concept, like creating a custom CD cover.

STEP 1   Create a new file for CD cover art by selecting **File > New** to open the New document dialog box. From Preset choose Photo, set the width and height 4.974 inches, and click OK.

This gives you a file that is slightly larger than needed so you can create artwork with a bleed. Press Ctrl+R/⌘+R to view your rulers and add guides at 1/8 inches in from each of the four sides.

STEP 2   Copy an interesting high-resolution photo into the CD file to use as the main picture for the cover art, and then add two text layers for the name of the band and the album title, in the font, size, and color of your choice as illustrated in Figure 89-1.

Once you have the text aligned the way you like it, select the band name layer and select **Layer > Rasterize > Type**.

Figure 89-1

STEP 3   In a separate window, open an image that has strong lines and angles pointing in different directions, such as a shot of a skyscraper, apartment building, or busy interior scene. Click the Threshold icon on the Adjustments panel and shift the white slider to the left until the image has a good balance of black and white tones. Figure 89-2 shows a busy, angular image before (top) and after (bottom) adding the Threshold adjustment.

Figure 89-2

STEP 4   Merge the image and threshold layers by selecting both layers and choosing Merge Visible from the Files panel menu. To choose the black parts of the merged layer, choose **Select > Color Range**, and when the dialog box opens, click your cursor on a black area within your open document, and click OK. Press Ctrl+C/⌘+C to copy the selection, switch back to the open CD file, and press Ctrl+V/⌘+V to paste the selection.

STEP 5   Ctrl+click/⌘+click the newly pasted threshold layer thumbnail to reselect all the black pixels, select the rasterized band name layer, and press Delete/Backspace to delete the selected pixels from the text layer. Now press Ctrl+D/⌘+D to deselect and hide the visibility of the threshold layer. Figure 89-3 shows the completed CD cover layout with the distorted effect on the text.

Figure 89-3

365

VII

IMAGE RETOUCHING AND RESTORATION

TECHNIQUE 90

CLEANING UP DIGITAL NOISE

NOISE IS A term used to describe the irregular brightness, color, and pixelation that occurs within digital images photographed in low light or with long exposures. You'll also find noise in images that have been poorly optimized as well as in scanned halftone images. Noise is the digital equivalent of film grain; however, this kind of digital noise is rarely seen as aesthetically pleasing. Although most people use the Median and Reduce Noise filters to remove grain, these tools often remove too much of the sharpness and definition within the image. A smarter way to reduce noise is to blur the noisy pixels within the channels.

STEP 1   Open a noisy file in Photoshop, like the one in Figure 90-1, which clearly has a noticeably mottled irregular pattern of grain and brightness.

Figure 90-1

STEP 2   Switch over to the Channels panel and click on the Red channel. This should automatically hide the visibility of the other channels so that you can see how much noise is present in just the reds. Select **Filter > Blur > Surface Blur**, and when the dialog box opens, adjust the radius to between 5 and 10 px and the threshold to between 3 and 15 px. The actual amount depends upon the quality and amount of noise in your particular image. For instance, with the example photo shown here, the radius was set to 5 and the threshold set to 4. Once you have found the right settings for this channel, click OK to close the dialog box.

STEP 3   Now select the Green channel, which will automatically hide the visibility of the other channels, and select **Filter > Blur > Surface Blur**. Again, when the dialog box opens, adjust the sliders to reduce the noise and click OK.

Repeat this process on the Blue channel and then click the RGB channel to view the full-color image. Figure 90-2 shows a detailed view of the example image before (left) and after (right) fixing the noise through the channels.

> HINT: Although this method can remove much of the graininess from your digital file, if the original image quality is poor to begin with, you may still see some noticeable grain after this process.

Figure 90-2

STEP 4   If your image seems a little bit too light or too dark, you can adjust the luminosity without having to use a Curves or Levels Adjustment.

With the RGB channel still selected in the Channels panel, Ctrl+click/⌘+click the RGB channel thumbnail to load the image's luminosity onto the Clipboard, and then press Ctrl+J/⌘+J to create a new layer filled with the luminosity selection.

Switch over to the Layers panel and you will see this new layer, which you can label as *luminosity*. To lighten the image, change this layer's blending mode to Screen, or to darken the image, change the blending mode to Multiply or Darken. Figure 90-3 shows a comparison of the original image (top), the corrected image (middle), and the image with the extra luminosity layer (bottom).

Figure 90-3

91
TECHNIQUE

REMOVING DUST AND SCRATCHES

IF YOU HAVE ever looked through a batch of old photographs from the 1970s or earlier, you'll probably notice quite a few of the images are plagued by varying amounts of dust and scratches. The dust typically comes from there being dust on the negative during the printing process, whereas the scratches are on the surface of the printed image, usually caused by mistreatment or neglect in storage over the years. If there is not a lot of dust and scratches on an image, you can selectively remove individual instances with the Clone Stamp or Healing Brush tools. However, for images with a significant amount of dust and scratches, you need a bolder solution.

STEP 1   Open an old photo in Photoshop that contains some noticeable areas with dust and scratches, like the circled areas in the picture shown in Figure 91-1.

Figure 91-1

STEP 2   Press Ctrl+J/⌘+J to duplicate the image onto a new layer, and then select **Filter > Noise > Dust and Scratches**. When the dialog box opens, set the radius to 1 and the threshold to 0, and then click OK. As you can see, the dust and scratches are gone, but the image appears a little bit blurry now.

STEP 3   With the duplicate layer selected, click the Add Layer Mask icon at the bottom of the Layers panel and then select the mask thumbnail. Press B to select the Brush tool, choose a 200 px soft-edged brush from the Options bar, and paint with black to erase parts of the blurred image and reveal the sharpness in the underlying original image layer. Figure 91-2 shows the example image after removing dust and scratches.

374

Figure 91-2

HAND TINTING PHOTOS

BEFORE THE INVENTION of color film, photographers who wanted color images had to painstakingly hand tint their black and white photographs with colored paints and dyes. Today hand tinting is more of a fine art technique that gives any photo an old-fashioned, charming, nostalgic feel.

STEP 1 Open an old image in Photoshop, like the example in Figure 92-1, and perform any restoration tasks that are needed, such as adjusting the Levels, removing dust and scratches, and repairing rips and tears, so that you start with a nice clean black and white (or toned) image.

Figure 92-1

HINT: If you would like to work from a newer color photo, convert the image into black and white by clicking the Black & White icon on the Adjustments panel and adjusting the settings as needed. Then select both the duplicate and Adjustment layers and merge them using the Merge Layers command in the Layers panel menu.

STEP 2   Press Shift+Ctrl+N/Shift+⌘+N to create a new layer, name the layer *Color*, and at the top of the Layers panel, change this layer's blending mode to Hard Light and the opacity to 21%.

STEP 3   Change the foreground color to the first color tint you'd like to apply to your image. Select the Brush tool (B) with a medium-sized soft-edged brush and gently paint over the various areas of the image.

HINT: If your photograph contains people, work from large areas to small, starting with overall skin and clothing, and then moving onto details such as lips, eyes, cheeks, teeth, and other features.

Change the colors, brush size, brush hardness, flow, and opacity as needed while you work, and feel free to put each area (lips, face, dress, and so on) on its own layer to allow for more fine-tuned adjustments. Erase any mistakes as you go along with the Eraser tool (E).

STEP 4   When you have finished adding all the tints to your image, add a touch of overall warmth to the image by clicking the Photo Filter icon on the Adjustments panel, choosing the Sepia filter, and adjusting the density to about 50%.

HINT: For an added boost of realism, use the Dodge and Burn tools to add some natural looking shadows and highlights.

If tinting a recent photo, add noise (choose **Filter > Noise > Add Noise**) to make the image look a little more aged. Figure 92-2 shows the original example image after it has been restored (left) next to the finished hand-tinted version (right).

Figure 92-2

TECHNIQUE 93

REMOVING BLEMISHES

IF BEAUTY IS in the eye of the beholder, we can all use a little help in the beauty department from time to time when it comes to improving our skin tone. Why let people look at our flaws when we'd rather have them focus on our better features like our piercing eyes, distinguished nose, or charming smile? Retouching results look best when performed in two stages with different tools. You'll use the Clone Stamp tool to retouch areas along the edges of the face, near the ear, and along the hairline, and the Spot Healing brush for touching up sections within the face and neck.

STEP 1   Open your image in Photoshop and zoom into the first area if the face that needs retouching. Press Shift+Ctrl–N/Shift+⌘+N to create a new layer so you're not working destructively on the original and label the new layer *retouching*.

STEP 2   First, you'll take care of skin blemishes within the face and neck. Select the Spot Healing Brush tool (J), which allows you to remove blemishes by blending the surrounding skin areas. On the Options bar, select Sample All Layers and choose a soft-edged brush slightly bigger in diameter than the area you are correcting. For best results, you should also verify that the Content-Aware option is selected (for CS4 or earlier, choose Proximity Match).

> *HINT: For the Healing Brush blending mode at the top of the Options bar, consider toggling between the Normal and Lighten settings. Normal produces good results when touching up areas with variable tones, whereas Lighten will only affect the darker areas being retouched while the lighter surrounding pixels remain the same.*

To use the brush, simply click once directly on top of the blemish, mole, or scar. Magic! Repeat throughout the face as needed. Figure 93-1 shows a close up of section of skin before (left) and after (right) retouching with the Spot Healing brush.

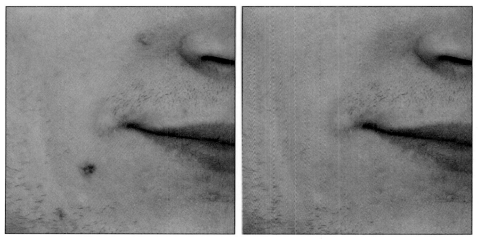

Figure 93-1

STEP 3   Next, you'll tackle areas along the edges of the face, ear, and hairline. Select the Clone Stamp tool (S) with a soft-edged brush slightly larger than the area to be corrected. Before you can use the tool, however, you need to sample nearby pixels to "paint" with. To do that, Alt/Option+click once on the source location, and then click or click+drag to paint over the blemish.

Repeat this process along the perimeter of the face and hairline as needed. This technique is also useful for cleaning up scratches and tears in scanned images, smoothing out wrinkles, and removing moles, stray hairs, and freckles.

381

STEP 4   To smooth out the overall tone of the skin, Alt+click/Option+click on the New Layer icon (or select **Layer > New > Layer**) to call up the New Layer dialog box. Give your layer a name such as *smoothing*, change the mode to Overlay, check the Fill with Overlay-neutral Color (50% gray) option (which only becomes visible after changing the mode to overlay), and click OK. Using a small (175 px) soft-edged brush with the foreground color set to white, gently paint over any parts of the skin that have irregular tone. If needed, reduce the opacity of this layer or adjust the blending mode to Soft Light. Figure 93-2 shows an example of an image before (left) and after (right) retouching.

Figure 93-2

TECHNIQUE

94

REMOVING UNDER EYE CIRCLES

THE FRESHEST FACES in fashion, television, and the movies have clear complexions, bright eyes, full lips, and even skin tone. What you will rarely see, however, are any under eye circles; those bothersome patches of slightly darkened skin right below the eyes. No matter their cause—whether it is lack of sleep, hydration, allergies, or diet—under eye circles make a person look tired. Thankfully, with Photoshop, you can remove all evidence of under eye circles in your images.

STEP 1   To begin, open an image in Photoshop and press Ctrl+J/⌘+J to create a duplicate of the original layer.

There are several tools you can use to digitally remove under eye circles, as you'll soon discover, but by far the most natural-looking method involves the use of the healing brush.

STEP 2   Select the Healing Brush tool (B), choose a medium-sized brush with 50% hardness, and set the brush's blending mode to Lighten. Then Alt/Option+click to sample an area just below the under eye circle and click and drag to paint across the under eye. Repeat this process for the other eye, and if needed, adjust the opacity of the layer down by about 5–10%. Figure 94-1 shows an original image before (top) and after (bottom) retouching using this method.

Figure 94-1

STEP 3 Here's a brief outline of how to use some of the other tools to remove under eye circles on a duplicate of the original layer:

- Brush Tool: Select the Brush tool (B), choose a soft-edged brush and set the brush opacity to 20%, sample the subject's skin color with the Eye Dropper tool (I), and paint across the under eye area. When finished, change the layer's blending mode to Lighten.

- Clone Stamp Tool: Select the Clone Stamp tool (S), choose a medium-sized soft-edged brush, and set the brush's opacity to 50%, set the duplicate layer's blending mode to Lighten, sample an area just below the under eye circle area by Alt/Option+clicking, and paint across the under eye region. When finished, adjust the layer's opacity to between 65%–95%.

- Patch Tool: Select the Patch tool (J), set the patch sampling option to Source on the Options bar, drag a selection around the area to be fixed, and then drag that selection to a smooth area of skin just below it. Upon releasing your mouse, the patch destination will fill the patch source selection. Immediately select **Edit > Fade Patch** to reduce the opacity of the effect. Repeat this process on the other eye until satisfied with the results. When finished, adjust the layer's opacity to about 50%.

Figure 94-2 shows a comparison of the original image to each of these methods.

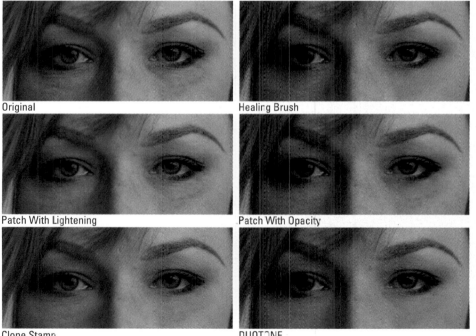

Original

Healing Brush

Patch With Lightening

Patch With Opacity

Clone Stamp

DUOTONE

Figure 94-2

LIGHTENING THE IRISES

IF EYES ARE the windows to the soul, it's understandable that magazines would benefit (and sell more magazines!) from making the eyes on the models and celebrities on their covers more piercing and alluring to look at. To achieve this special clear-eyed look, retouchers use is a simple technique to lighten the irises.

STEP 1   Open the image you'd like to retouch in Photoshop, press Ctrl+J/⌘+J to duplicate the background layer, and zoom into one of the eyes.

STEP 2   With the duplicate layer selected, press O to select the Dodge tool and, on the Options bar, choose a small, soft-edged brush. Set the range to Shadows and set the exposure to 30%. Slowly and carefully trace the outer edges of the iris with your brush in a single stroke (if possible), taking care to avoid the pupil in the center of the eye, as illustrated in Figure 95-1 (the retouched image is on the right).

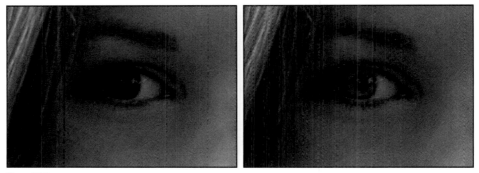

Figure 95-1

STEP 3   Repeat this process with the other eye on the same layer, and then change the layer's opacity to 70%. Figure 95-2 shows an example of a full image before (top) and after (bottom) retouching.

387

Figure 95-2

TECHNIQUE 96

CHANGING EYE COLOR

WE ALL KNOW that colored contact lenses can change the color of your eyes, but if the thought of wearing contacts, undergoing surgery, or having someone cast an eye-color-changing spell on you makes you squirm, different colored eyes can still be yours with Photoshop.

STEP 1   Open the image you'd like to retouch in Photoshop, press Ctrl+J/⌘+J to duplicate the background layer, and zoom into the face so you can clearly see both eyes.

STEP 2   Select the Elliptical Marquee tool (M) and make a round selection around the iris of the first eye. After releasing your mouse, hold down the Shift key so you can add to the selection by dragging a second round selection around the second eye, as illustrated in Figure 96-1.

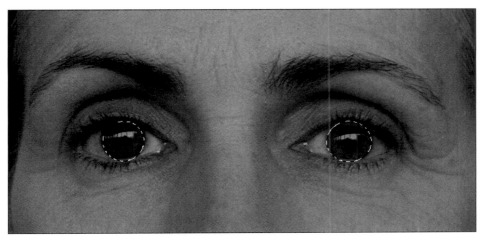

Figure 96-1

STEP 3   Click the Add New Fill or Adjustment Layer icon on the bottom of the Layers panel and select Solid Color. When the Color Picker dialog box opens, select the desired replacement color for the eyes such as a light blue with the hex value of #73c2e7, and click OK. Now change the layer's blending mode to Soft Light to show the underlying shadows and textures of the iris.

STEP 4   To clean up the hard edges of the added color, which you can see an example of in Figure 96-2, select the mask of the Color Fill adjustment layer and select the Brush tool (B) with a 30 px soft-edged brush. On the Options bar, set the brush mode to Normal and the opacity to 42%, and then paint with black as the foreground color to hide or "paint away" the outer edges of the color around the irises. Paint away any additional color that overlaps the eyelids or sits directly over the pupils.

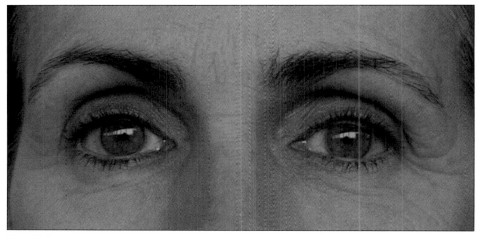

Figure 96-2

STEP 5   If you accidently paint away too much color, switch the foreground color to white and paint again to add the color back in. Figure 96-3 shows a full image before (top) and after (bottom) changing the eyes from brown to blue.

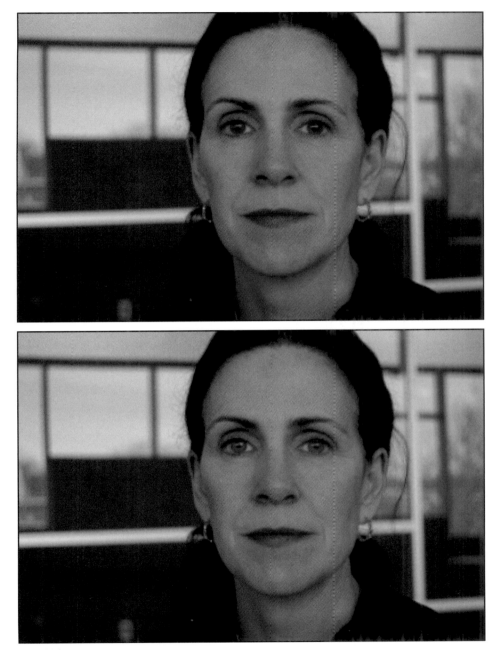

Figure 96-3

97
TECHNIQUE

BRIGHTENING AND SHARPENING EYES

EYES ARE OFTEN the first thing we notice about a person. They can generally tell us a lot about a person's character, such as whether the person is friendly, honest, trustworthy, and reliable, and whether they got enough rest last night. With a few simple steps in Photoshop, you can reduce the appearance of blood vessels, make the whites brighter, and add a hint of overall sharpening. This will help give the eyes a sparkle, making the person appear more friendly, alive, awake, healthy, and happy.

STEP 1   Open the image you'd like to retouch in Photoshop, press Shift+Ctrl+N/ Shift+⌘+N to create a new layer, name the layer *whites 1*, and zoom into the face so you can clearly see both eyes. Figure 97-1 shows an example of expressive yet somewhat bloodshot eyes.

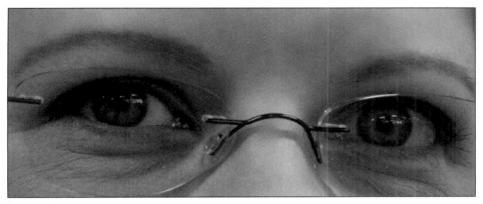

Figure 97-1

STEP 2   Press B to select the Brush tool and use the Options bar to select a small, hard-edged brush with the opacity set to 50% and the blending mode set to Color. Use the Eye-dropper tool (I) to sample a color from the whites of the eyes (don't be alarmed if the sampled color looks gray!) and paint over any visible blood vessels in each eye. When finished, lower the opacity of this layer to 70%.

STEP 3   To make the whites of the eye a little bit whiter, click Shift+Ctrl+N/Shift+⌘+N to add another new layer and label this layer *whites 2*. Then grab the Brush tool (B), and with the opacity set to 30% and the blending mode set to Normal, sample a white from the eye again and paint with that color over the eye whites. When finished, lower this layer's opacity to 65%. Figure 97-2 shows an example of how the first (top) and then the second (bottom) painted layers can change the appearance of blood vessels.

STEP 4   To change the color of the irises, follow the steps in Technique #96, "Changing Eye Color." Otherwise, to simply lighten the eyes a touch, add a new layer with the blending mode set to Soft Light and, with the foreground color set to white, paint with a small, soft-edged brush with the brush opacity set to 25% over the irises to lighten them ever so slightly. Then paint with black to darken the pupils and the smallest outer edge of the irises.

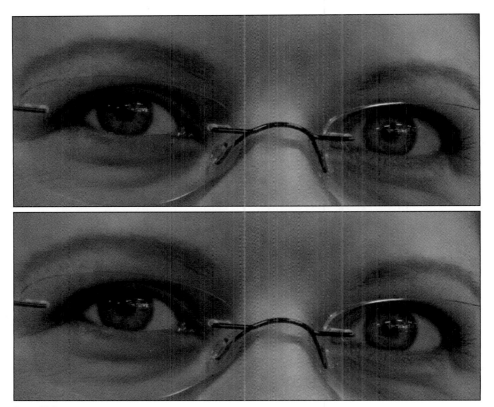

Figure 97-2

STEP 5   Select the Lasso tool and make a selection around both the eyes from under the eyes to just over the brows. Press Shift+Ctrl+C/Shift+⌘+C to copy all the visible layers, and then press Ctrl+V/⌘+V to paste the selection onto its own layer. Label this layer *sharpen eyes*.

Select **Filter > Sharpen > Unsharp Mask**, set the amount to 125%, the radius to 3 px, the threshold to 8 levels, and then click OK. Now Alt+click/Option+click the Add Layer Mask icon at the bottom of the Layers panel, set the foreground color to white, and use a 45 px-sized soft-edged brush to reveal the sharpness around the eyes and lashes. Figure 97-3 shows the finished effect below the original version.

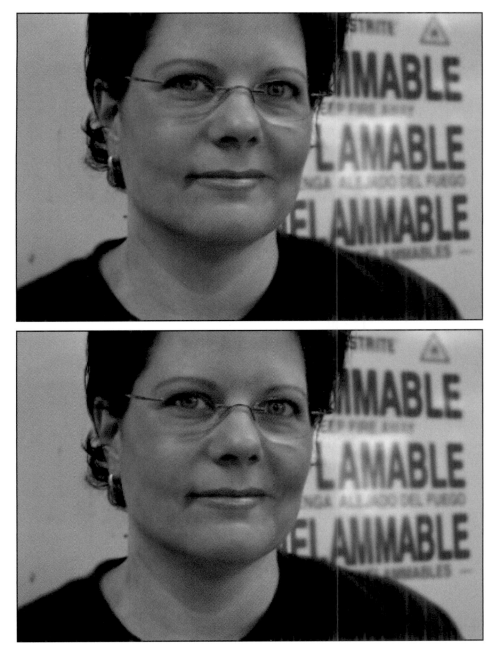

Figure 97-3

TECHNIQUE 98

WHITENING TEETH

AS WE GET older, the white outer layer of enamel on our teeth begins to wear away, revealing the underlying layer, called dentin, which tends to appear more yellow. Of course, teeth stains can also be caused by tobacco, coffee, tea, and certain foods. Sadly, even when we take proper care of our "pearly whites" with regular teeth cleaning, whitening toothpastes, and home bleaching treatments, most teeth whitening treatments are only temporary. Digitally speaking, however, you can quickly brighten any smile with a Hue/Saturation Adjustments layer.

STEP 1   Open the image you'd like to retouch in Photoshop and zoom into the mouth area.

STEP 2   Use the Magic Wand tool (W) or any of your preferred selection tools to make a careful selection of all the teeth in your image. Don't worry too much, though, about being 100% precise, as you can touch up the selection area in a later step.

STEP 3   Click the Hue/Saturation icon on the Adjustments panel, then click on the panel's drop-down menu where it says Master, and select the option called Yellows. Next, adjust the saturation slider all the way to the left so that the value box says -100. Now click on the panel's menu again where it says Yellows, change it back to Master, and then adjust the Lightness slider to +10. Figure 98-1 shows the Adjustments panel settings for Yellows and Master along with a view of the Layers panel.

Figure 98-1

STEP 4   To make any fine-tune corrections to the selection area around the teeth, select the Hue/Saturation layer's mask and a 35 px soft-edged Brush tool (B), and paint with white to reveal more areas of the mask. If you need to hide some areas of the mask, paint with black.

Finally, you can either leave the opacity of this layer set to 100% or take it down to 70% or 80% to let a little bit of the original image show through. Figure 98-2 shows an example of teeth before (top) and after (bottom) digital whitening.

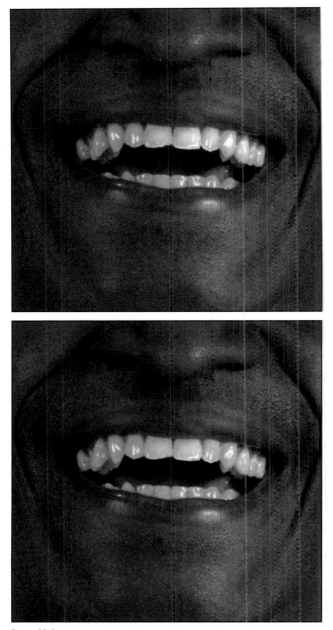

Figure 98-2

TECHNIQUE

99

REDUCING WRINKLES AND SMOOTHING SKIN

RETOUCHING SKIN IS often thought of as one of the most difficult tasks to perform well in Photoshop because not only is there is no one right way to do it, but there is also no precise template to follow to get it right, and that's because every image is completely different. As you learned in Technique #93, "Removing Blemishes," and Technique #94, "Removing Under Eye Circles," there are often several ways to retouch different areas of the face. Even so, that should not stop you from trying to give the faces in your images smoother, even-toned skin for a more youthful, fresh, and well-rested appearance.

STEP 1   Open the image you'd like to retouch in Photoshop and press Ctrl+J/⌘+J to duplicate the background layer. You're going to use the Surface Blur filter to smooth out the layer while preserving edges and areas with contrast and detail, as illustrated by the retouched image at the bottom in Figure 99-1.

Figure 99-1

STEP 2   Select **Filter > Blur > Surface Blur**, set the radius to somewhere between 5 and 20, set the threshold to somewhere between 10 and 20, and then click OK.

STEP 3   Alt+click/Option+click the Add Layer Mask icon at the bottom of the Layers panel to add a mask that completely hides the blurred layer, select that mask, and with a 35 px soft-edged Brush tool (B), paint with white to reveal areas of the blurred layer over the wrinkled areas. If you accidently reveal too much of the underlying layer, paint with black to hide those parts. When you're satisfied, reduce the layer's opacity to 65%.

The retouched image on the right in Figure 99-2 shows another example of reducing wrinkles and smoothing skin. As you can see, what tends to look most natural is not to completely get rid of wrinkles, but rather to subtly conceal the most prominent areas, thereby giving the completion an overall healthy glow.

Figure 99-2

100
TECHNIQUE

RETOUCHING WITH LIQUIFY

DIGITAL PHOTO RETOUCHING is a special talent that requires a thorough knowledge of Photoshop and hours of practice, patience, dedication, and skill. Although some retouching tasks are relatively easy, such as smoothing the skin, removing blemishes, brightening eyes, and whitening teeth, the toughest tasks involve what amounts to digital plastic surgery. A good part of digital retouching involves improving areas that people generally want to fix without having to change their diet or visit a gym. For instance, with Photoshop you can shrink a double chin, slim down a waistline, fill out the bust, or plump up the lips. Believe it or not, the best tool for this type of work is the Liquify filter.

STEP 1   Open the image you'd like to retouch in Photoshop, press Ctrl+J/⌘+J to duplicate the background layer, and zoom into the area that needs retouching. For example, the image in Figure 100-1 shows a model in a bikini. While her figure is already quite nice, you can easily retouch it to have more of an appealing hourglass shape.

Figure 100-1

STEP 2   With the duplicate layer selected, select **Filter > Liquify** to open the Liquify dialog box. Along the left edge of the screen, select the Pucker tool (S), and along the right side adjust the tool options as follows: set the brush size to 250, the brush density to 50, the brush pressure to 100, the brush rate to 38, and the turbulent jitter to 50.

Place the crosshair of your brush just a little bit inside the edge that you want to "bring in" and then make a series of quick clicks along that edge to "pull" the pixels inward. Repeat this process along the other edges as needed. If you happen to make a mistake, click the Reconstruct button to undo or press Restore All to revert the file to its original state and try again.

STEP 3   To make an area plumper, such as the lips or bottom, use the Bloat tool (B) with a slightly smaller brush size in a similar fashion. When you are satisfied with your figure-reshaping edits, click the OK to exit the dialog box. Figure 100-2 shows the same model after retouching.

Figure 100-2

Index